ON FOOT GUIDES

VENICE WALKS

D0902045

ON FOOT GUIDES

VENICE WALKS

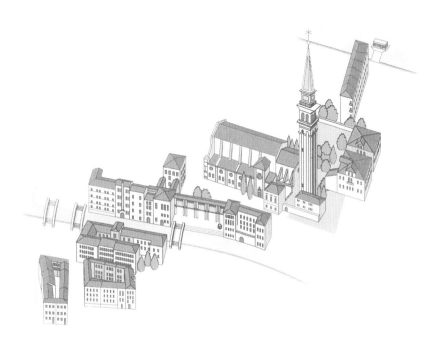

Jo-Ann Titmarsh

DUNCAN PETERSEN

gpp®
travel
Guilford, Connecticut

Copyright © 2008, 2010 Duncan Petersen Publishing Ltd

Conceived, designed and produced by
Duncan Petersen Publishing Limited
C7, Old Imperial Laundry
Warriner Gardens, London SW11 4XW
United Kingdom

Published in the USA by
Globe Pequot Press
Guilford, Connecticut

UK ISBN-13: 978-1-903301-52-4
UK ISBN-10: 1-903301-52-1
US ISBN-13: 978-0-7627-4845-7
US ISBN-10: 0-7627-4845-1

A CIP catalogue record for this book is available from the British Library.
Library of Congress Cataloging-in-Publication Data is available.

The right of Jo-Ann Titmarsh to be identified as the author of this work has been asserted by her in
accordance with the Copyright, Designs and Patents Act 1988.

Conceived, designed and produced by
Duncan Petersen Publishing Ltd

Editorial Director Andrew Duncan

Editors Jacqui Sayers, Rollo de Walden

Maps Julian Baker, Peter Bull and Anthony Duke

Photographs Francesco Allegretto, Jo-Ann Titmarsh

Thanks also to Lydia Allegretto, Kate Davies and Gillian Price

Printed by C&C Offset Printing, China

**Visit Duncan Petersen's travel website at
www.charmingsmallhotels.co.uk**

CONTENTS

Exploring Venice on foot

Compact, car-free, and packed with charming, narrow passageways, Venice is *the* city to explore on foot. Although viewing the city afloat on its canals offers a whole new dimension, gondolas or water taxis are expensive and clumsy ways of getting around. You will gain much more of a feel for this incomparable place by ambling down its dark, narrow alleys and ducking under its many covered passageways. No bigger than New York's Central Park, Venice nonetheless offers a lifetime of endlessly fascinating walking possibilities. The efficient waterbus (*vaporetto*) service takes you to and from the start and end points of our walks.

Thanks to draconian urban planning laws and lack of space, Venice has little new architecture to remind you that this is a functioning contemporary city, and not just an Italian Renaissance theme park. The exceptions are a handful of buildings by Venetian architect Carlo Scarpa and the Cassa di Risparmio building in Campo Manin by Pier Luigi Nervi and Angelo Scattolin (see walks 9 and 10). Wherever you walk, you will find architectural treats – even the smallest squares contain something of interest.

Venice is divided into six neighbourhoods, known as *sestieri*: San Marco, Santa Croce, San Polo, Dorsoduro, Cannaregio and Castello. There are three districts on either side of the Grand Canal, which curves in a backward 'S' through the heart of the city. The labyrinthine nature

---

HOW THE MAPPING WAS MADE

A small team of specialist cartographers created the maps digitally in Adobe Illustrator. The footprint of the buildings is drawn first, then the width of the streets is artificially increased in order to give extra space for the buildings to be drawn in three dimensions. Next, the buildings are added, using aerial photography as reference. Finally the details of the buildings and the colour is added - the first very time consuming, the second less so because digital drawing programmes allow it to be automated.

of the city can make it difficult to find your way, but the unique aerial-view (isometric) mapping used in this guide is the answer to your prayers: it is easier to use than flat mapping because you can locate yourself by the look of the buildings, as well as by the street plan. The unique look of the maps brings *calli* (streets), *campi* (squares), *fondamente* (watersides), individual buildings and even

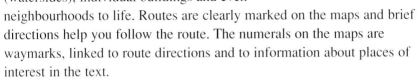

neighbourhoods to life. Routes are clearly marked on the maps and brief directions help you follow the route. The numerals on the maps are waymarks, linked to route directions and to information about places of interest in the text.

The purpose of the walks is to introduce you, district-by-district, to every aspect of this amazing city, from the most grandiose *basilicas* to the humblest of dwellings. We've deliberately excluded St Mark's Square, except in the introductory walk. The Arsenale is also not featured, though glimpses of its imposing walls and turrets can be had from one of the walks. However, you will rarely be far from these two areas that represent Venice's erstwhile financial power and naval supremacy, and in any case, seeing them properly needs two separate expeditions.

There are many confusing variations in the spelling of place names in Venice, and some streets *campos* and bridges often have more than one name, usually the Venetian and Italian vernacular. In the text that describes the walks, Jo-Ann Titmarsh has copied the spellings seen on the ground, in order to reassure you that apparently odd spellings are okay. In contrast, our isometric maps generally use spellings found on conventional sheet maps of Venice, in order to make you aware of the alternatives.

The 12 walks are in-depth explorations. Even if you think you know Venice pretty well, they'll enable you to discover plenty of hidden delights. The best cafés, restaurants and shops are indicated along the way. The walks can generally be completed in less than two hours, though a morning would allow more time to explore. If you choose to make the most of what the area has to offer, it could last all day. If you complete all of the walks, you will come to know Venice very well indeed.

HOW TO USE THIS BOOK

The area covered by the walks stretches from Dorsoduro in the south to the Church of Santi Giovanni e Paolo in the north, and from the Church of the Frari in the west to the island of San Pietro di Castello in the east of the city.

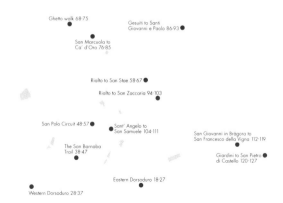

Ghetto walk 68-75

Gesuiti to Santi Giovanni e Paolo 86-93

San Marcuola to Ca' d'Oro 76-85

Rialto to San Stae 58-67

Rialto to San Zaccaria 94-103

San Polo Circuit 48-57

Sant' Angelo to San Samuele 104-111

San Giovanni in Brágora to San Francesco della Vigna 112-119

The San Barnaba Trail 38-47

Giardini to San Pietro di Castello 120-127

Eastern Dorsoduro 18-27

Western Dorsoduro 28-37

Using the maps

The route of each walk is clearly marked on the map, with arrows to point you in the right direction. The guide also tells you where the walk starts and ends, indicating the nearest *vaporetto* stop, which is never more than a few minutes' walk away. Numerals on the maps correspond to the numerals in the text, marking the start of each section of the walk. They will help you to maintain your bearings. **Bold print** alerts you to points of interest on the route that follow in the order mentioned. Bold is also used to indicate other interesting places nearby, such as museums, galleries, statues, restaurants, bars or shops. Where relevant, closing days are given in brackets. For more information on admission to sights, see page 14.

LINKING THE WALKS

Many of the walks are within easy reach of each other and part of the fun of linking two walks in Venice is that you can make use of the waterbuses. For example, you can hop across from Ca' d'Oro at the end of **Heart of Cannaregio** to Rialto Mercato for the **Food Walk**. **Underneath the Arches** finishes at San Tomà and you can hop across the water to Sant'Angelo to begin **Central San Marco**. **Salute, Accademia and Zattere** leads you to the Salute boat stop and you can catch a *vaporetto* to San Zaccaria (just two stops away) to commence the **Saints all the Way** itinerary. When you finish the **Food Walk** at Campo San Stae you are one stop away from San Marcuola and the start of the **Heart of Cannaregio** route. The **Fresh Air and Simple Pleasures** route ends at Sant'Alvise and you can catch a boat to the Fondamente Nuove to commence **Miracle Church**. **Marco Polo Heartland** takes you to San Zaccaria, from whence you can start **Saints all the Way**. Or, after **Marco Polo Heartland**, catch a boat from San Zaccaria to Giardini (or walk east along the embankment), to begin **Green Venice**.

   If you use the gondola ferries (for the bargain price of 50c), when you finish **Central San Marco** at San Samuele, you can catch the gondola to Ca' Rezzonico to set off on the **Stars and Bars** walk. Alternatively, **Underneath the Arches** finishes at San Tomà and you can catch a gondola across the water to Sant'Angelo to begin **Central San Marco**, though you will need a Venice map to lead you to your starting point, which is slightly to the west of the gondola stop.

In August, the weather in Venice can be unbearably hot and humid, with temperatures frequently hitting the mid-30s and humidity well over 70 per cent, and so many Venetians traditionally shut up shop and head to the mountains. Winters can be extremely harsh, with Siberian winds from the east, though generally the weather is cold and damp. The best seasons for a visit are spring and autumn, though beware *acqua alta*. Literally meaning 'high water', this phenomenon occurs mainly in the rainiest months of November and March and sees the city flooded at its lowest points.

WHEN TO USE THIS BOOK

Most of the walks can be enjoyed throughout the year, but some – particularly those which include parks – are more fun to walk in fine weather in spring.

Summer walks

• **Fresh Air and Simple Pleasures**: this is a great walk for the spring, when the gardens are blooming and most lush. It is not so great in the summer, when the sun beats down unremittingly whilst walking the length of the Fondamenta di Cannaregio. However, if you start early, you will avoid the sun and be rewarded with a leafy haven at the end of the walk.

• **Green Venice**: commencing at the Giardini and ending in the shade of San Pietro di Castello, this is a great walk for the summer and is relatively unpopulated by the hordes of tourists cramming into other parts of the city. Catching a *vaporetto* at San Pietro will cool you off after your walk.

• **Underneath the Arches**: taking you down dark alleys and under countless archways, this is a great walk when the sun is at its most scorching.

• **Miracle Church**: starting from the north-facing Fondamente Nuove and heading down some hidden streets, this walk offers solace from the searing heat during the summer months.

• **Stars and Bars**: a great walk, particularly on summer evenings when the outdoor tables along the way will be heaving with Venetian young things and tourists enjoying outdoor life.

• **The Food Walk**: at Rialto market the cornucopia of fruit and vegetables in all their colourful array, as well as the silver glint of the fish, is a dazzling sight in summer.

Winter walks

• **Salute, Accademia and Zattere**: in winter, it is customary for Venetians to take their after-dinner stroll along the Zattere, soaking up the weak rays of the winter sun. A hot chocolate at Faggiotto is a must. Watch out for flooding, though.

• **The Old Industrial Area**: beginning and ending on the Zattere, you can take advantage of one of the few places in Venice that get some direct sunlight in winter.

• **Heart of Cannaregio**: the long stretches of canal banks could in theory turn you into a heat stroke victim in the summer. In winter, these open spaces offer a sense of space and

light as an antidote to the gloomy weather.

• **Marco Polo Heartland:** though Venice is rarely quiet, there are fewer tourists in winter. This walk takes you through the heart of the city and you may find it more peaceful in winter months.

WEEKEND WALKS

• **Salute, Accademia and Zattere:** though this walk can of course also be done during the week, Tuesdays should be avoided when the Peggy Guggenheim Collection is closed, along with many of the surrounding shops.

• **Saints all the Way:** with many of the finest eateries closed on various weekdays, I suggest that you head for this route on a weekend.

• **Miracle Church:** most of this walk is more peaceful at weekends, although the Fondamente Nuove comes to life, with florists lining the embankment touting their wares to those heading to the cemetery.

WEEKDAY WALKS

• **The Food Walk:** don't attempt this walk on Sundays and Mondays, when the fish market is closed. Saturdays see locals doing their weekly shop. On other days, the market is buzzing, but not brimming over.

• **Fresh Air and Simple Pleasures:** the Ghetto museum and synagogues are closed to the public for the Shabbat on Saturdays. During the week, particularly in the mornings, the parks are quieter.

• **Green Venice:** the wonderful fruit and vegetable boat in Via Garibaldi, plus the local fishmongers and local shops are closed at weekends. The bars and restaurants cater to local workers, so you are better off taking this itinerary on weekdays.

• **Marco Polo Heartland:** the post office, a Venice institution, is shut on Sundays, as are many of the shops and eateries. Didovich pastries are not to be missed.

• **The Old Industrial Area:** this walk has a livelier local feel during term-time weekdays, when architecture students are rushing to lessons or grabbing a bite in local bars.

DIVERSIONS

You'll come across many a street, *fondamente* or bridge closed for restoration. These *deviazione* are marked by large yellow signs and generally take you to the point you want to reach, or else close to it. Don't be alarmed: they are usually easy to follow.

Stars and Bars: some of the sights are shut on Tuesdays, but many of the fabulous boutiques are closed on Sundays, so choose your weekday carefully when considering this itinerary.

WALKS FOR KIDS

Venice is a notoriously difficult city for children. The sheer volume of museums and churches makes it a toddler's hell. However, the following routes could be more enjoyable for small people:

• **Fresh Air and Simple Pleasures:** This route has few churches, begins and ends with a park, and has a children's bookshop in the middle. There may even be the possibility of a swim at the end. And the history of the Ghetto could appeal to an older child or a teenager.

• **The Food Walk:** starting at Rialto market, most children will enjoy gazing at the writhing sea creatures on sale. The walk also leads to the Natural History Museum, which, though small, offers a Jurassic moment for kids. There are plenty of pit stops along the way for hungry/thirsty/tired nippers.

• **Green Venice:** with the play park at Giardini and the quiet streets and watersides, this is a great walk for children. There are plenty of hidden detours that children will enjoy discovering.

• **Marco Polo Heartland:** get the kids to mail your postcards from the superlative post office close to Rialto Bridge, then check out the Marco Polo second-hand bookstore for bargain books in English. The tall tales of

Marco Polo's travels can come to life whilst visiting his neighbourhood, and the Palazzo Querini Stampalia shows kids what a patrician home looked like.

• **Salute, Accademia and Zattere:** the marvellous Peggy Guggenheim Collection organizes children's workshops on Sundays in both English and Italian. For information check the website: www.guggenheim-venice.it.

GETTING TO VENICE
British Airways flies direct from Gatwick to Venice Marco Polo Airport and easyJet flies to the same airport from its main UK destinations. BMI Baby has regular flights to Marco Polo from Heathrow, whilst Ryanair flies in to Treviso, with a direct bus service to Venice. You can now fly direct to Venice from the US (New York, Atlanta and Philadelphia).

GETTING AROUND
The ACTV (Venice's transport authority, www.actv.it) offers a regular and efficient boat service throughout the city and islands, and it runs an excellent mainland bus service. The website has an English page with timetables for all routes online. Punch in the relevant data and out will come full details on how to proceed.

ACTV waterbuses
Tourist tickets are expensive if you purchase single tickets (€6 for a one-way fare, valid for one hour after punching it in the ticket machine), so if you are planning to use the waterbuses during your stay, you may want to buy special tickets. There are various options available, such as the 12, 24, 36, 48 and 72-hour options, costing from €13 to

€30. If you just want to cross the Grand Canal, the *traghetto* tariff for tourists is €2. Tickets can be purchased at most ACTV stops and from *tabacchi* (newsagents) with an ACTV sign in the window.

Tourist cards
The Venice Card is a special tourist ticket that you can buy either for public transport, toilets and baby-changing facilities (blue card) or all of the above, plus free admission to the Musei Civici, Fondazione Querini Stampalia, the Jewish Museum and free access to Chorus Pass churches, if you buy the 2- or 7-day (orange) card. See www.venicecard.it for tariffs.

Water taxis
You can arrive in Venice in style from Marco Polo Airport by catching a water taxi, though this is expensive at €90. The main water taxi ranks are situated at Piazzale Roma, Santa Lucia train station, near the Rialto *vaporetto* stop, next to the San Marco Valaresso *vaporetto* stop and Giardini ex Reali (near San Marco). However, water

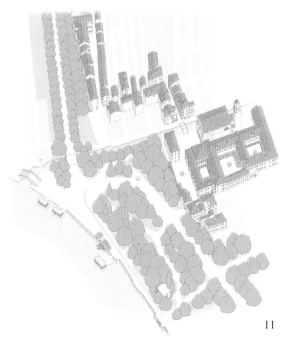

taxis are prohibitively expensive with a minimum charge of €70 for a single passenger. They are best value when travelling as a group (up to 12 passengers, max). Hotels will often add a 10 per cent mark-up if you book through them. To book a taxi, call 041 716 922 (24-hour service). You can hail water taxis, though it is best to go to a taxi rank or hotel water entrance. There is a €10 surcharge after midnight and taxi drivers only accept cash. See www.venezianamotoscafi.it for details.

Gondolas
Official gondola stops can be found at the following: Fondamenta Bacino Orseolo (situated behind St Mark's Square); outside the Danieli Hotel on Riva degli Schiavoni; by the San Marco Valaresso *vaporetto* stop; outside the railway station; by Piazzale Roma bus terminal; by the San Tomà *vaporetto* stop; in Campo Santa Sofia (near the Ca' d'Oro *vaporetto* stop), by the Hotel Bauer in Campo San Moisè; on Riva del Carbon on the San Polo side of Rialto Bridge. The Gondola Board (tel 041 528 5075/www.gondolavenezia.it) sets the prices for gondolas, which are as follows: 8am-7pm, €80 for 40mins; 7pm-8am, €100 for 50 mins; €50 for each additional 30 mins. Gondola prices are for up to six people. These are the prices established by the Board and *gondolieri* are not allowed to overcharge. You can call the Board to complain if you feel you have been overcharged. Most *gondolieri* speak English and will point out places of interest and offer a little local history during the ride. Singers can be arranged at an extra cost.

Gondola ferry service
The gondola board offers a ferry service across the Grand Canal. These ferries require you to stand up on a gondola and are excellent value at 50 cents per person. They run between San Toma' and Sant'Angelo, San Samuele and Ca' --Rezzonico, Pescheria and Santa Sofia, Riva del Carbon and Riva del Vin, Santa Maria del Giglio and Salute, providing a quick and easy short cut across the city. (The San Marcuola-Fontego dei Turchi ferry service was closed at time of going to press for restoration work.)

TOURIST INFORMATION
APT (Azienda Promozione Turistica di Venezia) tourist information counters are open daily (excluding Christmas and New Year) and supply maps, lists of events, accommodation, guidebooks, information about guided tours and much more. You can find them at:
• Marco Polo Airport, tel 041 541 58 87 /529 87 11. Open 9.30am-7.30pm.
• Piazzale Roma, ASM Garage, tel 041 241 14 99. Open 9.30am-1pm, 1.30-4.30pm.
• San Marco, 71 F, Piazza San Marco, tel 041 529 87 11. Open 9am-3.30pm.
• San Marco 2, Giardini Reali, tel 041 529 87 11. Open 10am-6pm.
• Santa Lucia Railway Station, tel 041 529 87 11. Open 8am-6.30pm.
• Lido, Gran Viale Maria Elisabetta 6A, tel 041 526 57 21. Open 9am-12.30pm, 3.30-6pm, June-Oct.
Alternatively, check out the Tourist Office website at www.turismovenezia.it

Disabled travellers
Venice is an extremely difficult city for people in wheelchairs. There are around 400 bridges and only a very few have wheelchair ramps. Many of the buildings are more than five hundred years old, making them difficult to adapt for wheelchair users, with

elevators a rarity. However, although difficult, Venice is not impossible for the disabled and slowly the city is trying to adapt and to cater for all needs. Wheelchair users can use all ACTV boats without a problem and boat conductors are always ready to offer a hand when boarding and disembarking, which can be problematic when tides are exceptionally high or low.

Not all hotels have rooms accessible by wheelchair and you should always check with hotels before travelling. The APT (tourist information centre) provides a map showing bridges with wheelchair ramps and accessible public W.C.s, though tourists should be aware that these don't always work. Keys for operating the automated ramps are available from the APT offices. Before leaving, go to the Venice City Council website (www.comune. venezia.it-informahandicap) or write to them at informahandicap @-comune.venezia.it for information on visiting Venice for disabled travellers. Outside of Venice itself, Lido beach has W.C.s accessible by wheelchair on the private beaches, so if you hire a beach umbrella or beach hut you then have access to these facilities. The Lido, the cemetery island of San Michele, as well as Torcello, Burano and Murano otherwise have W.C.s accessible by wheelchair, indicated on tourist maps provided for disabled travellers.

Theatre tickets

Though not offering much in the way of nightlife, Venice is a hive of culture, with theatres dotted throughout the city. The three main theatres provide a variety of performances. Venice's famous opera house,

La Fenice, arisen from the ashes for the third time, has a full programme of opera, ballet and concert performances, though you should book well in advance. Address: San Marco 1965, Campo San Fantin. Box office: 041 24 24, www.teatrolafenice.it.

The Teatro Malibran was Venice's principal theatre during La Fenice's lengthy restoration after the fire of 1996. Now it acts as a complement, rather than competition, to its more famous sister. Many of the Biennale Dance performances take place here, as well as opera and live music performances. Address: San Marco, Campiello del Teatro. For box office and programme, see the La Fenice website.

The Teatro Carlo Goldoni is considered by many to be the most beautiful theatre in Venice. Its season mainly consists of performances of Italian classics, with Goldoni an obvious attraction. It also hosts pop and rock concerts. Address: San Marco 4650 B, Calle Goldoni. Box office: 041 240 20 14 , www.teatrostabileveneto.it.

Tour guides

You can ask the tourist office for a list of private tour guides. Or, contact the *Cooperativa Guide Turistiche* (Tourist Guide Coop) at San Marco 750, calle Morosini de la Regina (tel 041 520 90 38 /www.guidevenezia .it. Open June-Aug 9am-1pm, 2-6pm Mon-Fri; 9am-1pm Sat; Sept-May 9am-5pm Mon-Fri; 9am-1pm Sat. This cooperative offers a tour guide service in a multitude of languages, including English. You can book in advance (and this is advisable in high season).

Boat trips

Alilaguna, which also offers an airport service to various locations around Venice, offers organised group tours of Murano, Burano and Torcello. These multi-lingual boat trips are good value without being heavy on the culture and history. However, it's a great way to sit back and enjoy the watery experience of the Venetian lagoon and its wonderful islands. For further details, visit the website at www.alilaguna.it.

Useful publications

Un Ospite di Venezia is a free magazine providing information about events in the city. An online version is available at www.ospitedivenezia.it. There are a host of tour guides about Venice. Two of the best are *Time Out Venice* and *Eyewitness Venice*. For the best online advice about hotels, see www.charmingsmallhotels.co.uk, or, for a bigger selection, buy *Charming Small Hotel Guide Italy*, £14.99 published by Duncan Petersen.

Lost property

For items left on ACTV transport contact the ACTV head office at Santa Croce, Piazzale Roma (tel 041 272 21279) open 7am-7.30pm daily. For items found by rubbish collectors or members of the general public, contact the Comune (city council) at San Marco 4136, riva del Carbon (tel 041 274 8225) open 8.30am-12.30pm Mon-Fri and 2.30-4.30pm Mon and Thur. Santa Lucia Train Station has its own lost property office, next to track 14 (tel 041 785 531), for all items found on local trains, on platforms or in the station building. For luggage lost on flights to Marco Polo Airport, go to the Arrivals Hall lost luggage office (tel 041 260 92 22), open 24 hours daily.

Ambulance 118
Police (English-speaking helpline) 112
Fire Brigade 115
Coastguard 1530
If you need to report a theft, missing person or any other matter for the police, go to a local police station. You'll find these at: Castello 4693 A, Campo San Zaccaria t 041 520 4777; Castello 5053, Fondamenta di San Lorenzo 041 271 5511; Santa Croce 500, Piazzale Roma 041 271 5511

Hospital accident and emergency departments (ask for the *pronto soccorso*) are open 24 hours daily and must treat you free of charge in an emergency. Some doctors speak English. Venice's main hospital is: Ospedale Civile, Castello 6777, Campo Santi Giovanni e Paolo. Tel: 041 529 4111; casualty: 041 529 4516.

On the Lido, the hospital is: Ospedale al Mare a Lungomare D'Annunzio 1, Lido. Tel 041 529 5234.

There are pharmacies all over Venice, and are easy to spot with the green cross above the entrance. Otherwise ask your hotel for the address of the nearest one. You can check *Un Ospite di Venezia* magazine for a list of chemists open in the evening.

Opening hours

Most **major attractions** open at 9am or 10am to 6pm (sometimes later), with Monday closing. Most attractions have different opening times depending on the season. Most of the major churches are open from 9am-5pm in summer.

Most **banks** are open 8.30am-1pm or 1.30pm, and sometimes 2.45pm-3.45pm, Mon-Fri. They are closed on public holidays, and have much shorter hours the day before.

Shops are generally open between 9am

and 10am until 7.30pm Mon-Sat, sometimes closing for an hour or two at lunch. Some close on Monday. But many shops are open all day, and Sunday opening is also common in the more populous tourist areas around Rialto and St Mark's. Most supermarkets open at 8.30am and close at 7.30-8pm Mon-Sat, though some are open on Sundays.

Food markets are open for business at 7am and close around 12.30pm, although the Rialto tourist market (non-food) is open all day. **Pharmacies** (*farmacia*) are usually open 9am-1pm and 4-8pm Mon-Sat. Late-night pharmacies and Sunday openings are available on a rotation system and a sign on the pharmacy door will direct you to the nearest one open.

Bars and **cafés** tend to vary in their hours. However, although snacks may be served throughout the day, hot meals in cafés are usually served at times similar to restaurants: midday-2.30pm and 7-10.30pm.

Public holidays

Many museums, sights, banks and shops are closed on public holidays. The following is a list of public holidays with the Italian translation in brackets:

1 January
6 January (*Epifania*)
Easter Day (*Pasqua*)
Easter Monday (*Pasquetta*)
25 April (*Festa della Liberazione*, also *Festa di San Marco*, patron saint of Venice)
1 May (*Festa del Lavoro*)
2 June (*Festa della Repubblica*)
15 August (*Ferragosto*)
1 November (*Ognissanti*)
21 November (*Festa della Salute*, only in Venice)
8 December (*L'Immacolata*)
25 December (*Natale*)
26 December (*Santo Stefano*).

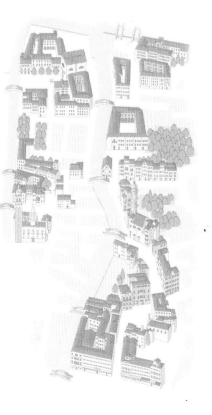

Introducing Venice on Foot

This route is an introduction to Venice, helping you to find your bearings and introducing you to some of the landmarks around the city, many of which you will come across in later walks. The itinerary takes about a day and loops around the city, traversing the Grand Canal twice before returning to the starting point. Predominantly keeping to the major thoroughfares, this is the walk to do if you are only in town for the day and want to take in as many landmarks as possible whilst keeping the risk of getting lost to a minimum.

For those with little time and stamina, a great way to see the city is by boat, catching the No. 1 *vaporetto* either from Piazzale Roma bus and car terminal or Santa Lucia railway station all the way down the Grand Canal, crossing the lagoon to Lido, before heading back.

Start at **Santa Lucia** railway station, the logical starting point for many visitors and easy to reach for those arriving by road. From the steps of the station building you can see **Ponte degli Scalzi**, one of the four bridges spanning the Grand Canal. Turning left, passing the **Scalzi Church** with its pretty Baroque façade, head east down **Lista di Spagna**, one of Venice's busiest streets, running through the heart of the Cannaregio district. This road leads to **Campo San Geremia** with its unassuming church, striking palace and entrance to the local park (see **Fresh Air and Simple Pleasures**, page 68).

Continuing east, cross **Ponte delle Guglie** and continue along **Rio Terà San Leonardo**, past the colourful market stalls (and signs for the **Jewish Ghetto**, see page 73). Crossing **Rio di San Marcuola**, the road becomes **Rio Terà Maddalena**, with the intriguing **Church of Santa Maddalena** in a picturesque *campo* on your right (see **Heart of Cannaregio**, page 78). Across the bridge, the road now becomes **Strada Nuova**, teeming with shops, street vendors, locals and tourists. Before the next bridge, to your left is **Church of San Felice** and over the bridge, further down to the right, is the magnificent Gothic **Ca' D'Oro** (both in **Heart of Cannaregio**, page 85). The street widens into **Campo Santa Sofia**, with a ferry stop from which you can take a gondola across the water to the Rialto market. The street comes to an end in leafy **Campo dei Santi Apostoli**.

From here walk south, across the bridge and under the *porticoes*, following the signs to Rialto, through **Campiello Corner** and down **Calle San Giovanni Crisostomo**, with the **Teatro Malibran** and **Marco Polo's** home behind the church to your left (see **Marco Polo Heartland**, page 96). Cross **Ponte de l'Olio**, going past the impressive **Fontego dei Tedeschi**, now the main post office (**Marco Polo Heartland**, page 96). This takes you to **Campo San Bartolomeo**, with **Rialto Bridge** to your right and the statue of Goldoni in the centre of the square. Just before the **Church of San Salvador**, turn left into the **Mercerie**, a long winding alley full of elegant boutiques since Renaissance times. Wending your way over **Ponte dei Bareteri** and down **Mercerie dell'Orologio** leads you under the **Torre dell'Orologio** (clock tower) into jaw-dropping **St Mark's Square**. To your right, at the end of the *piazza*, is the **Museo Correr** and to your left is the **Basilica di San**

Marco, its four bronze horses standing guard in the *loggia*. Next door to the Basilica is the intricate façade of the **Doge's Palace**, once seat of the Venetian Republic senate. Directly opposite is the **Biblioteca Marciana**, the city library built by Florentine Renaissance architect, Jacopo Sansovino. Alongside it is the *campanile*, painstakingly rebuilt after collapsing in 1922. Between these buildings, overlooking the lagoon and the mystical island of San Giorgio Maggiore, are two columns, one bearing a chimera and the other Saint Theodore, Venice's original patron saint. **Caffè Florian**, the oldest coffeehouse in Europe, has outdoor seating, or stand at the bar at the back of the café to enjoy a less overpriced drink.

Leaving the *piazza*, head west from the Museo Correr down **Salizada San Moisè**, crossing the bridge and heading down **Via XXII Marzo**, the Bond Street of Venice. Keeping to this path, with the Grand Canal's watery presence a few paces away to your left, takes you through some pretty squares. Of particular interest are **Santa Maria del Giglio** and **Campo San Maurizio**. From here you are a short walk away from **Campo Santo Stefano**, one of the liveliest and loveliest squares in Venice (see **Central San Marco**, page 110), with plenty of bars and cafés should you need a break.

Head south out of the square and cross the wooden **Accademia Bridge**. At the bottom of the bridge are the **Gallerie dell'Accademia** containing a surfeit of art treasures (see **Salute, Accademia and Zattere**, page 21). Turn right, down **Calle Corfù** and cross the pretty canal into **Calle Toletta**, past a multitude of bookshops, until you reach **Campo San Barnaba** (see **Stars and Bars**, page 43). Continuing north west, cross **Ponte dei Pugni** and you will reach one of the prettiest *campi* in town: **Campo Santa Margherita** (**Stars and Bars**, page 44). This is an ideal spot in which to take a breather: there are bars and restaurants, many with outdoor tables, but also a supermarket and park benches, should you want a picnic.

From the *campo* go down **Calle della Chiesa** and cross the white bridge into **Campo San Pantalon**. Follow the road to the right of the church until you come to **Tonolo**, the most famous patisserie in Venice. Turn left, then immediately right and go over the bridge with the **Scuola Grande di San Rocco** in front of you and the much-filmed **Campiello di Castelforte** to the left (**Stars and Bars**, page 45). Take the alley to the left of the bridge into **Campo San Rocco** to reach the *Scuola* and church of the same name. Further to the right is the glorious Gothic masterpiece, the **Basilica Santa Maria Gloriosa dei Frari** (see **Underneath the Arches,** page 51).

From the Church of San Rocco, walk down **Campo Chiovere** and turn left into **Calle Chiovere**. Head straight on until you reach **Campo dei Tolentini**, with Carlo Scarpa's ingenious entrance to the University Institute of Architecture to your left and the Tolentini Church around the corner. Turn right in the *campo* and walk down the pretty canal bank of **Fondamenta dei Tolentini**. At the end of the street, turn right on to **Fondamenta San Silvestro Piccolo** and the Grand Canal. Just after the imposing church steps is **Ponte degli Scalzi**, taking you back to the railway station and your starting point. For those travelling by road, at **Campo dei Tolentini**, take the bridge to the left of the square and go straight on until you reach the **Piazzale Roma** bus terminal and car park.

ERRA DELLA MADDALENA

STRADA NUOVA

Ca' d'Oro

Campo Dei Santi Apostoli

Campo Santa Sofia

Rialto Bridge

Campo S Bartolomeo

MERCERIA DELL'OROLOGIO

Piazza San Marco

Campo Santo Stefano

C. LARGA 22 MARZO

Red dots show locations of the 12 walks in this guide.

Salute, Accademia and Zattere: Eastern Dorsoduro

Though it's hard to avoid the hordes in Venice, this walk offers a stroll down some of the quietest *calli* in town whilst serving up some of its most renowned sights. Here you can find collections of Renaissance masters standing alongside purveyors of contemporary art, not to mention some architectural gems. The eastern side of Dorsoduro (literally meaning 'hard back') has seen a decline of the local population, with wealthy foreigners snapping up properties. While this has created a dearth of grocery

Detail of a relief from the Santa Maria della Vizitazione.

C. CORFU GAMBARA

FONDAMENTA PRIULI

FONDAMENTA MARAVEGIE

CAMPO SAN TROVASO

C. NUOVA S. AGNESE

PISCINA FORNER

C. D. CHIESA

FOND.

RIO TERRE ANTONIO FOSCARINI

FONDAMENTA VENIER

FONDAMENTA BRAGADIN

FONDAMENTA ZATTERE AI GESUITI

CANAL DELLA GUIDECCA

FONDAMENTA ZATTERE

shops and other services, it has boosted the district's newfound role as Venice's very own SoHo, with art galleries abounding. The route will take you on a loop from the magnificent Baroque Salute Church, down narrow alleys and along wide sunlit canal banks, past well-known sites and lesser treasures, before leading you back to your starting point. Should you wish to curtail the walk, there are plenty of *vaporetto* stops *en route*. This itinerary is best avoided on Tuesdays, when the Peggy Guggenheim Collection, and thus many of the adjacent galleries and shops, are closed. And beware of *acqua alta* (flooding) – the low-lying Zattere could see you wading rather than walking this route.

▶ STARTS
Salute Church.
Nearest *vaporetto* stop:
Salute.

■ ENDS
Salute church. Nearest *vaporetto* stop: Salute.

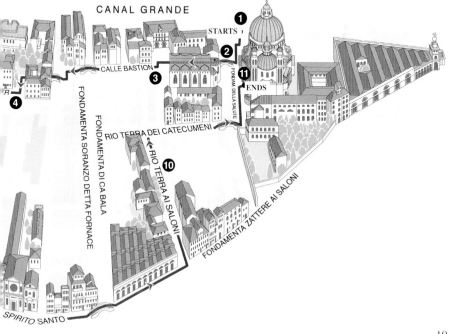

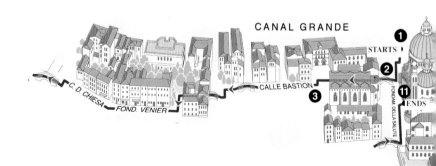

1 Hopping off the *vaporetto* at the **Salute** boat stop, you will find yourself standing before the **Santa Maria della Salute Church** at the tip of Dorsoduro. After plague swept through the city in 1630, decimating a third of the population, in 1631 the Venetian Senate voted to erect a church to give thanks to the Madonna for its eradication, with work starting on Longhena's masterpiece in the same year. This wedding-cake church is home to works by both Titian and Tintoretto, but don't miss the painting above the high altar depicting *Venice Kneeling before the Virgin and Child* with the plague, in the form of a hideous crone, being hounded from the city. Each year on November 21st, Venetians still pay homage to the Virgin with a pilgrimage to the church while vendors sell candyfloss and balloons along the way.

Corner of building on Calle di San Cristiforo.

2 Crossing the wooden bridge closest to the Grand Canal leads you to **Calle Abazia**. The abbey in question once owned houses in this area, providing rent-free accommodation to the poor. Walking under the gloomy *sotoportego* of the abbey and down the alley, you reach **Campo San Gregorio** and its eponymous church. The date of the church is unknown, but there is evidence that it was already in existence in 897. It was rebuilt after a fire in 1105 and handed over to the Benedictine monks in 1140, before being deconsecrated in 1808. A stomach-churning story is associated with this church: one of its pilasters is said to house the skin of Marcantonio Bragadin, a Venetian soldier flayed alive by the Turks at Famagosta in 1571. His dermatological remains are now deposited at the Church of Santi Giovanni e Paolo. The *campo* also

Campo Abbazia.

houses one of Venice's leading glass designers: Giorgio Nason creates beautiful glass beads from which he designs contemporary jewellery, often integrating silver elements, designed by his wife, into the pieces.

Campiello Barbaro.

Santa Maria della Salute Church.

❸ Head down **Calle San Gregorio** then **Calle Bastion**, taking time to browse the windows of the many art galleries and Ermanno Nason's store with its wonderful menagerie of glass animals. Crossing **Ponte Barbaro** you descend into **Campiello Barbaro**, one of the prettiest and most diminutive *campielli* in the city. This verdant postage stamp offers a rear view of Ca' Dario, the crooked palace on the Grand Canal believed by Venetians to be cursed. After a breather on one of the park benches, head over **Ponte Cristoforo** and in a few moments you'll find the Peggy Guggenheim Collection (closed Tues) side entrance right in front of you. As well as Peggy's own private array of modern art, the Collection now holds regular exhibitions of modern and contemporary art. Relax in the garden and maybe eat something in the café before starting out afresh.

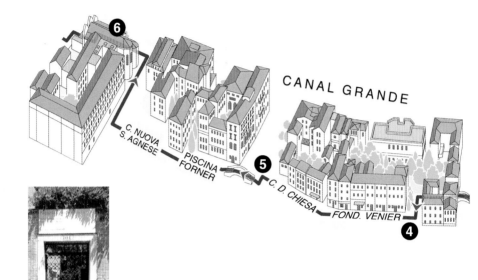

Doorway on
Fondamenta Venier.

4 Leaving the Guggenheim, take a right and follow **Fondamenta Venier** into **Calle della Chiesa**, which will take

Fondamenta Venier.

you to **Campo San Vio**, home to the Anglican **Church of Saint George**, where Sunday services are held. Head over the bridge and immediately to your right on the other side is **Palazzo Cini**, once home to Conte Vittorio Cini and now part of the foundation set up by the Conte in memory of his son, who died in a plane crash in 1949. Housing a cornucopia of porcelain and antiques on the first floor, the second floor is used for temporary exhibitions. Visits must be booked in advance.

Fondamenta Venier.

Grand Canal from Accademia.

⑤ From Palazzo Cini, continue down **Piscina Forner** and **Calle Nuova Sant'Agnese**. At the end of the street turn right and you will see the **Accademia Bridge** spanning the Grand Canal. Here, in **Campo Carità**, are the Accademia galleries, currently undergoing major restoration and expansion work to provide more exhibition space, a café and a museum bookshop (scheduled completion date 2008). This staggering collection includes all the Venetian heavyweights: Bellini, Titian, Tintoretto, Veronese and Tiepolo are just some of the great masters on show here. Though Venetians still bear a grudge against Napoleon, it is thanks to him that these galleries and the art academy exist.

Grand Canal as seen from the Accademia.

⑥ After an exhausting tour of the Accademia, you may be in need of sustenance. Leaving the Accademia turn left, and on the corner you will find **Caffé Belle Arti**, once the hangout of artists and now a favoured tourist haunt. Continue along **Calle Corfu Gambara** and then turn left on to **Fondamenta Priuli**, on one of the loveliest canals in Venice, **Rio San Trovaso**, more of which later. Crossing the first bridge you come to, turn left and you arrive at the amazing chocolate emporium, **Faggiotto**. Ask for an *espresso* of hot chocolate (made without milk) or, in summer, iced chocolate. Leaving the shop, keep the **Rio San Trovaso** on your left and continue more or less straight ahead to sleepy **Campo San Trovaso**. This is one of Venice's most charming – and

Calle Corfu.

most photographed – *campi*. The **Church of San Trovaso** boasts not one but two façades. Legend has it that the church was built on the borders of territory owned by two feuding families, both of which required a suitably grand entrance, hence the almost identical façades. However, it is neither the charming church nor the patch of grass with park benches that draws the camera-wielding crowds, but the **Squero di San Trovaso**, one of the few remaining gondola-building boatyards.

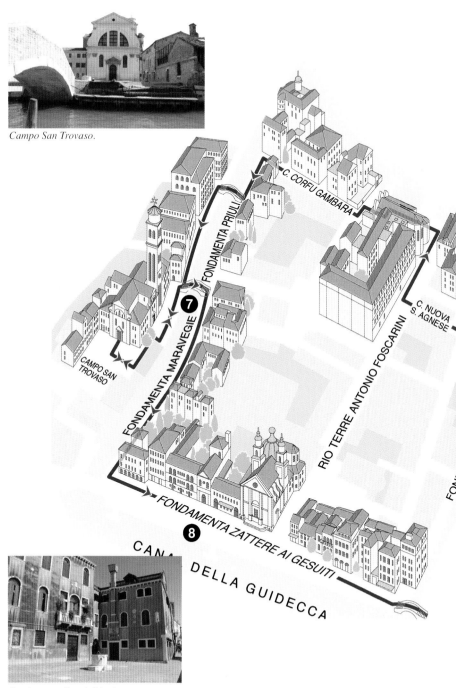

Campo San Trovaso.

C. CORFU GAMBARA

FONDAMENTA PRIULI

7

C. NUOVA
S. AGNESE

CAMPO SAN
TROVASO

FONDAMENTA MARAVEGIE

RIO TERRE ANTONIO FOSCARINI

8

FONDAMENTA ZATTERE AI GESUITI

CAN...

DELLA GUIDECCA

Fondamenta Sangiofoletti.

Squero di San Trovaso.

7 Retrace your steps back to the first bridge, cross and turn right on to **Fondamenta Nani** where you can enjoy a glass of *prosecco* and a snack at the justly famous **Cantinone Schiavi**. It is from this *fondamenta* that you can get your best shots of the *squero*. Head south to the end of the *fondamenta* and turn left back onto the **Fondamenta Zattere ai Gesuati,** where you will find the *vaporetto* stop for the Giudecca.

Statue at Gesuiti.

Façade of Gesuiti.

8 This vibrant stretch of the Zattere has two churches: **Santa Maria della Visitazione** and the **Gesuati**. Though the latter pulls in the visitors, thanks to the frescoed ceiling by Tiepolo, the former has a pretty façade – possibly designed by the great Renaissance architect Codussi – and a wonderful coffered ceiling. It is now the chapel of the *Istituto Don Orione*, which takes paying guests in the nearby cloistered ex-Domenican monastery.

Detail on wall of Campo San Barnaba.

Detail on wall of Campo San Barnaba.

❾ Moving east along the Zattere, and crossing yet another bridge, you come to the *Ex Ospedale degli Incurabili*. This hospital once cared for women with venereal diseases, but is now home to the more felicitous *Accademia di Belle Arti*. It is a vast complex, boasting a courtyard with a well in each corner. Past the **Church of the Spirito Santo** lie the **Saloni Ex Magazzini del Sale**. These 14thC warehouses once stored the city's precious salt supply, but now house rowing clubs and – at least during the *Venice Biennale* – provide exhibition space for visiting national pavilions.

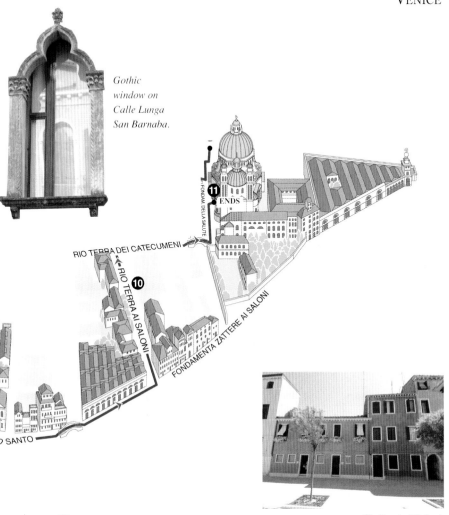

Gothic window on Calle Lunga San Barnaba.

Rio Terrà ai Saloni.

Calle Lunga San Barnaba.

⑩ After the Magazzini del Sale, turn left on to **Rio Terrà ai Saloni**. This was once a canal, but is now a pretty street with trees running down its centre. On the right-hand corner of this street and **Rio Terrà dei Catecumeni** stands the **Ex Ospizio**. This building originally housed 'infidels', or rather non-Catholics taken prisoner during Venetian incursions against the Ottomans. Though Ottomans had been present in Venice since at least 1099, the year of the first crusade, it was not until 1557 that the Senate decided to house them all under one roof. Turning right on to this charming *rio*, cross the bridge at the end and you will find yourself on the **Fondamenta della Salute**. Turn left and follow the canal bank back to ⑪ where you started.

The Old Industrial Area: Western Dorsoduro

Campezzo di San Sebastiano.

This area of Venice isn't high on most tourists' lists. Western Dorsoduro was historically proletarian, inhabited by fishermen and salt-pan workers. When the industrial revolution came they worked at the port and in the local cotton mill. The mill is now part of the University of Architecture and the port area is about to undergo extensive regeneration based on the work of architect Enric Miralles, yet despite this makeover in the offing,

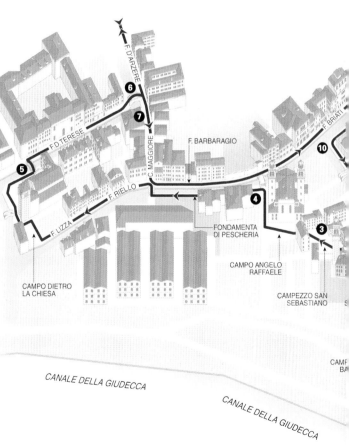

*Campo di
San Sebastiano.*

Western Dorsoduro is proud of its working class credentials. If you feel that you hadn't come to Venice to take an interest in industry, don't be put off. Even this ex-industrial zone boasts magical *campi* and stunning architecture. The route begins on the Zattere and takes you through one of the least visited parts of town, passing university buildings and delightful churches with the port area a hidden presence much of the way. This route is ideal for those for whom window shopping is anathema: the shortage of tourists means a lack of tacky glass shops and over-priced bars. On the other hand, foodies need not despair: the bars and restaurants along the way offer variety and quality, with menus that are a little different.

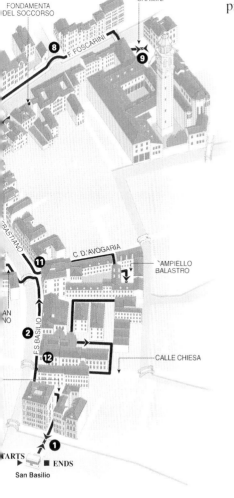

► STARTS
San Basilio *vaporetto* stop.

■ ENDS
San Basilio *vaporetto* stop.

29

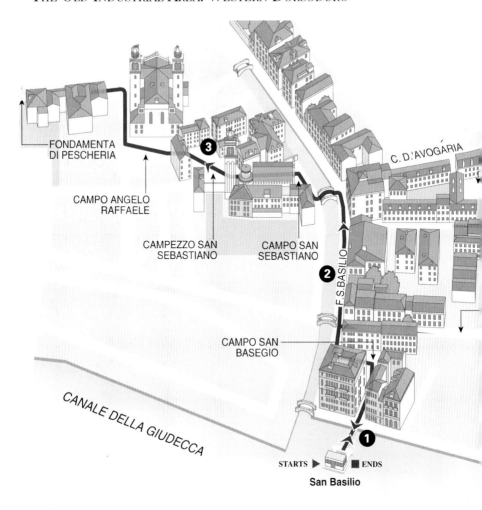

FONDAMENTA
DI PESCHERIA

C. D'AVOGÁRIA

CAMPO ANGELO
RAFFAELE

CAMPEZZO SAN
SEBASTIANO

CAMPO SAN
SEBASTIANO

F.S.BASILIO

CAMPO SAN
BASEGIO

CANALE DELLA GIUDECCA

STARTS ▶ 🚏 ■ ENDS

San Basilio

❶ San Basilio *vaporetto* stop overlooks the **Giudecca** and is directly opposite **Molino Stucky**, once a vast flour mill employing more than 1500 pasty-faced locals, before closing in the 1950s and standing derelict for 50 years. Now the new Hilton, it is a symbol of the city's regeneration and offers a foretaste of what may become of Western Dorsoduro. Looking at the mill, to your right is the vast

San Basilio vaporetto stop.

port area, also awaiting an architectural revamp, with a university campus on the cards. From here you can watch passengers disembarking from giant cruise liners and ferries. From the *vaporetto*, head straight into **Calle del Vento** and **Campo San Basegio** ('Basilio' vulgarised), a popular hang-out for students from the nearby university faculties.

2 Continue straight on to **Fondamenta San Basilio**, and cross the bridge to **Campo San Sebastiano**. The ex-convent adjacent to the church is now a university building, but the real treat here is the **Church of San Sebastiano**.

Fondamenta de San Basilio.

One artist was responsible for almost all of its frescoes and canvasses: Paolo Veronese. The story goes that Veronese (real name Paolo Caliari) was held prisoner in the church for an undisclosed offence. Starting in 1555, Veronese worked flat out, creating huge and vibrant biblical scenes, including, of course, *The Martyrdom of St Sebastian*. Veronese's relationship with the church does not end with this commission: both he and his brother are buried here. Other works include a late Titian.

Campo Sant'Angelo Raffaele.

3 Taking the alley alongside the church, and passing through **Campezzo San Sebastiano**, you reach the airy **Campo Angelo Raffaele**. To the left of the 14thC well is **Pane, Vino e San Daniele** (closed Wed), a charming *osteria* serving delights such as roast suckling pig. Ask for the one table in the cellar if you want privacy, or simply enjoy a drink at one of the many tables in the *campo*. The **Church of Angelo Raffaele** was probably founded in the 5th century, though the present building dates back to the 17th century. Worth seeing are the five panel paintings on the organ balustrade depicting the story of Tobias being cured of his blindness by the church's namesake, the archangel Raphael.

Sant'Angelo Raffaele.

CAMPIELLO
BALASTRO

CALLE CHIESA

The Old Industrial Area: Western Dorsoduro

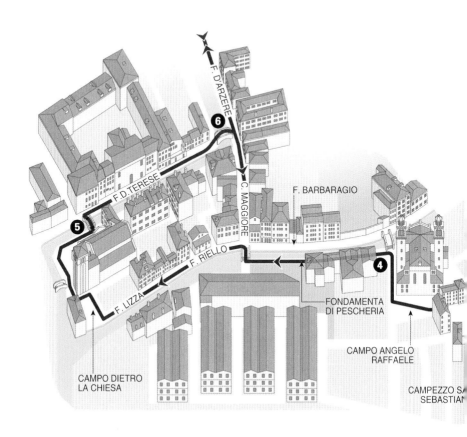

④ From the church, turn left on to **Fondamenta di Pescheria** with the port warehouses on your left. Crossing the water and turning left you find yourself in

Calle Drio la Chiesa.

Fondamenta Riello, then **Fondamenta Lizza**. At the end of the street, turn right into the charming and secluded **Campo dietro la Chiesa**. From here you witness two architectural gems. The first is the imposing **Cotonificio**, the cotton mill, built in 1883 and in its heyday employing more than a thousand workers. After standing empty from its closure in the 1960s, the building underwent a conversion and is now home to the IUAV (Venice University Institute of Architecture). It is also a successful example of how Venice could reinvent itself from industrial powerhouse and tourist trap to cultural hub. The second building is the more diminutive, but even more impressive **Church of San Nicolò dei Mendicoli**. One of the oldest churches in

Venice, and one of a handful retaining its 13thC Veneto-Byzantine structure, this church – literally meaning Saint Nicholas of the Beggars – once provided shelter to the homeless. It is also one of the only churches to have a ground-floor *loggia*. Restoration by the British charity, Venice in Peril, uncovered its original 7thC foundations.

n Nicolò dei Mendicoli.

⑤ From the north façade of the church, cross the bridge and turn right on to **Fondamenta delle Terese**. Local girl Maria Ferrazzo lost both her parents to the plague that ravaged Venice in 1630. Devoting her life to good deeds, in 1647 Maria founded the Carmelite convent situated on the *fondamenta*. Girls taking the veil there were nicknamed 'Teresa', hence the street name. Her followers remained here until 1810, after which the building became an orphanage.

CAMPO SAN
SEBASTIANO

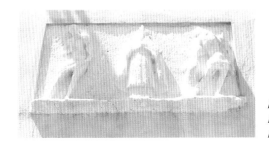

Detail on Fondamenta Lizza Fusina.

Ponte De Le Terese.

⑥ Crossing **Ponte De Le Terese**, you can detour left on to **Fondamenta dell'Arzere**, a wide and picturesque canal side. The Venetian term *arzere* refers to the extensive banks built to protect the area from water erosion. At the end of the street is the friendly **Vineria 'Al Canton'** bar (closed Sat) where you can grab a drink and a rest alongside the locals.

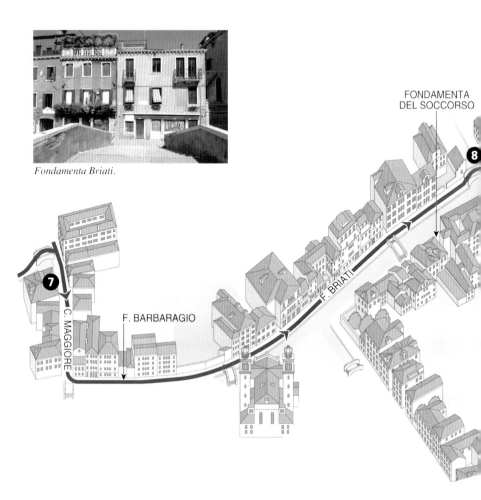

Fondamenta Briati.

7 Retrace your steps to **Corte Maggiore** and turn left on to **Fondamenta Barbarigo**, named after the patrician family whose palace was situated here. If you need lunch, **El Argentino**, the Argentinian restaurant just past the bridge, offers genuine Argentine beef and *impanadas*. Continuing along **Fondamenta Briati** you come to the Gothic **Palazzo Ariani,** with what Ruskin described as 'intricate but rude tracery' and a magnificent first-floor *loggia*. Further along, at the foot of **Ponte del Soccorso**, is **Bar Codroma** (closed Sun), a Venetian institution for spritz drinkers and late night revellers.

Fondamenta Briati.

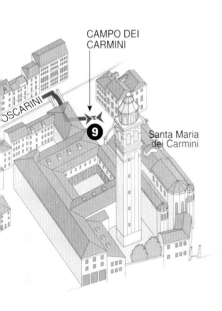

Detail on Chiesa dei Carmini.

8 Crossing Rio Briati on to **Fondamenta Foscarini**, go right over **Ponte Foscarini** into **Campo dei Carmini**. The Carmelite church **Santa Maria dei Carmini** was built in the 14th century, though it has endured many alterations over the centuries. Housing paintings by local boy Lorenzo Lotto and Cima da Conegliano, this imposing church also boasts a lofty bell tower and a beautiful side entrance with Byzantine reliefs on the eastern façade. Next door is the **Scuola Grande dei Carmini**, containing some magnificent frescoes by Giambattista Tiepolo. The Carmelites were so impressed with his work that he was made an honorary member of their brotherhood.

9 In Campo dei Carmini, with the church behind you, turn left into **Fondamenta del Soccorso**, home to the Baroque **Palazzo Zenobio** and **Collegio Armeno**. Built at the end of the 17th century and erstwhile home to the patrician Zenobio family, the palace was sold to Count Salvi and in 1850 to the Moorat Raphael Armenian school (named after its founding benefactors). It is also home to the Scottish Pavilion during the Venice Biennale. The palace garden provides a tranquil spot for relaxation and contemplation.

Fondamenta Briati.

Fondamenta di San Sebastiano.

⑩ Round the corner on to **Fondamenta San Sebastiano**. When you reach **Ponte San Sebastiano**, turn left into **Calle De L'Avogaria**. This quiet back street has one of the best restaurants in Venice: **L'Avogaria** (closed Tues). The architect owner, who designed the interior, is from Puglia (the Southern 'heel' of Italy) and his sister conjures up regional *pugliesi* dishes served in elegant, relaxed surroundings. The restaurant has a walled courtyard perfect on balmy evenings.

⑪ Continuing along Calle dell'Avogaria, detour left into **Corte Zappa**, where you will find **Teatro a L'Avogaria** (www.teatroavogaria.it), an experimental theatre founded in 1969 by director Giovanni Poli. The main route continues down **Ramo Balastro**, into **Campiello Balastro** and onwards down **Calle Balastro**, all named after a prominent family from the island of Torcello who set up home here in the 13th century. Leading into **Calle Chiesa**, this winding track is virtually unbeaten by tourists. You will see attractive two-storey homes with blooming window boxes and large communal gardens for use of residents of the apartment blocks.

Fondamenta di San Sebastiano.

Calle de L'Avogaria.

Fondamenta di San Sebastiano.

⑫ At the end of Calle Chiesa, turn left for the final stretch of **Fondamenta San Basilio**, popping into **Osteria da Toni** (closed Mon) for some typical Venetian fare (or at least a glass of wine) before reaching the **San Basilio** *vaporetto* stop.

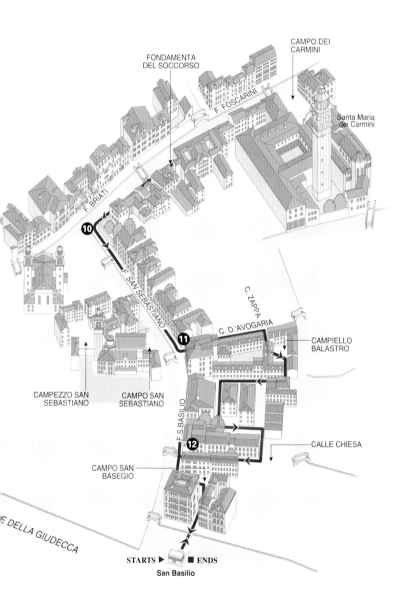

CAMPO DEI
CARMINI

FONDAMENTA
DEL SOCCORSO

F. FOSCARINI

Santa Maria
dei Carmini

F. BRIATI

10

F. SAN SEBASTIANO

C. ZAPPA

C. D'AVOGARIA

CAMPIELLO
BALASTRO

11

CAMPEZZO SAN
SEBASTIANO

CAMPO SAN
SEBASTIANO

F. S. BASILIO

CALLE CHIESA

12

CAMPO SAN
BASEGIO

E DELLA GIUDECCA

STARTS ▶   ■ ENDS

San Basilio

37

Stars and Bars:
The San Barnaba Trail

If the southern part of Dorsoduro offers tranquil streets that are off the usual tourist radar, by contrast north-eastern Dorsoduro is one of the liveliest spots in town. Università Ca' Foscari and IUAV(Venice University Institute of Architecture) attract students from Italy and abroad. Thanks to the students and a hard-drinking indigenous population, this circuit includes plenty of after-hour bars, often with open-air seating, as well as excellent eateries, concentrated around one of the principal hubs in Venice, Campo Santa Margherita.

Yet this route is not all about drinking and eating. From Ca' Rezzonico on the Grand Canal, you are led down picture-perfect canals, lured into ornate churches and taken to a pope's family home and a doge's palace. You'll get a taste of action, while also exploring more sober paths. And though this neighbourhood is not famous for its shopping, it offers everything from retro clothing to handmade masks and sumptuous fabrics – with not a chain store in sight.

▶ STARTS
Ca' Rezzonico.
Nearest *vaporetto* stop
Ca' Rezzonico.

Façade of Chiesa di San Barnaba.

Second courtyard in Ca' Foscari.

■ ENDS
Campo San Barnaba.
Nearest *vaporetto* stop:
Ca' Rezzonico.

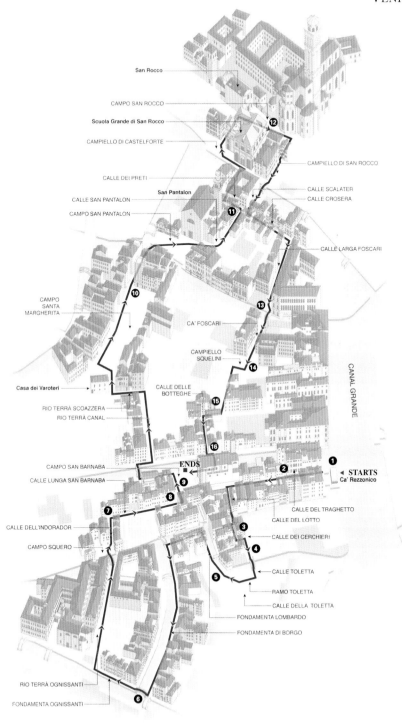

VENICE

San Rocco

CAMPO SAN ROCCO

Scuola Grande di San Rocco

CAMPIELLO DI CASTELFORTE

CALLE DEI PRETI

San Pantalon

CALLE SAN PANTALON

CAMPO SAN PANTALON

CAMPO
SANTA
MARGHERITA

Casa dei Varoteri

RIO TERRÀ SCOAZZERA
RIO TERRÀ CANAL

CAMPO SAN BARNABA

CALLE LUNGA SAN BARNABA

CALLE DELL'INDORADOR

CAMPO SQUERO

RIO TERRÀ OGNISSANTI

FONDAMENTA OGNISSANTI

CAMPIELLO DI SAN ROCCO

CALLE SCALATER
CALLE CROSERA

CALLE LARGA FOSCARI

CA' FOSCARI

CAMPIELLO
SQUELINI

CALLE DELLE
BOTTEGHE

CANAL GRANDE

ENDS

STARTS
Ca' Rezzonico

CALLE DEL TRAGHETTO
CALLE DEL LOTTO

CALLE DEI CERCHIERI

CALLE TOLETTA

RAMO TOLETTA
CALLE DELLA TOLETTA
FONDAMENTA LOMBARDO
FONDAMENTA DI BORGO

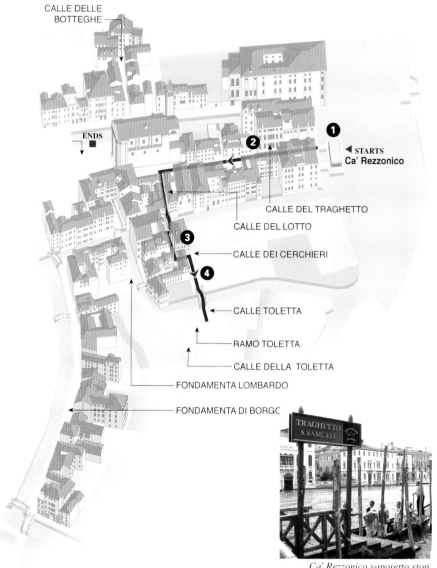

CALLE DELLE BOTTEGHE

ENDS

STARTS
Ca' Rezzonico

CALLE DEL TRAGHETTO

CALLE DEL LOTTO

CALLE DEI CERCHIERI

CALLE TOLETTA

RAMO TOLETTA

CALLE DELLA TOLETTA

FONDAMENTA LOMBARDO

FONDAMENTA DI BORGO

Ca' Rezzonico vaporetto stop.

1 There's a *vaporetto* stop here, but you can also get here on the *traghetto*, the stand-up gondola ferrying passengers across the Grand Canal, from San Samuele. Disembark at **Ca' Rezzonico** (closed Tues), one-time palace and now a museum of 18thC Venice. Designed by Pietro Longhena, who also designed the Salute, it was bought by the Rezzonico family, one of whom became Pope Clement XIII. The palace houses frescoes by Giambattista Tiepolo, Murano glass chandeliers, ornate period furniture and an impressive collection of 18thC art.

Calle del Traghetto.

❷ Heading straight down **Calle del Traghetto**, turn left into **Calle del Lotto**. These next few alleyways provide a peaceful haven away from the tourists jostling for space in the parallel streets. **Ponte di Malpaga** takes you over **Rio Malpaga**, both named after the nearby palace, only the walls of which now remain. Malpaga was the derogatory nickname given to the sea captain, Mattio Fantin, who, after battling abroad, took a tenth of his crew's earnings on reaching Venice. Adding insult to injury, the monthly salary was based on Fantin's personal 33-days-per-month calendar. Hence his moniker *malpaga* ('bad payer').

Calle dei Cerchieri.

❸ From **Calle Malpaga** you reach **Calle dei Cerchieri**, where you will see one of the best hidden – and cheapest – *osterie* in Venice: **Osteria Vini Padovani** (closed weekends). It is a real hole-in-the-wall establishment, with an exemplary wine list and small daily menu.

Calle Toletta.

❹ Directly opposite the restaurant walk down **Ramo dei Cerchieri**, crossing **Ponte Toletta** and going down **Calle Toletta** before turning right on to **Ramo Toletta**. From here you come to **Calle della Toletta**, a busy thoroughfare connecting the Accademia and Santa Margherita. The name of this street supposedly comes from *toleta* (Venetian dialect for 'small table'), used as a makeshift bridge to cross the canal. The most eye-catching aspect of this canal-turned-*calle* nowadays is the large number of bookstores and bars flanking its path, including **Ai Artisti** (closed Sun), serving some of the best bar snacks in Dorsoduro.

41

5 With the canal to your right, turn left on to **Fondamenta Lombardo**. A short walk down the *fondamenta* leads you to the picturesque **Fondamenta di Borgo** on the left. This sun-drenched street is virtually tourist free. If you do see any, they are probably on their way to **Locanda Montin** (closed Tue and Wed), which is halfway down the *fondamenta* coming from **Calle delle Turchette**. Though no longer one of the best restaurants in Venice, it does boast one of the most charming gardens in town.

Fondamenta degli Eremite.

6 At the end of Fondamenta di Borgo, cross the bridge on the right on to **Fondamenta Ognissanti**. Now home to a hospital and a university faculty, this complex was once a Cistercian convent. The nuns came to the authorities' attention in 1505, when one of the occupants was found to be pregnant with a priest's child. Turning right away from the *fondamenta*, go straight on along **Rio terrà Ognissanti** and over the bridge (taking note of the traffic lights on the canal) into **Campo Squero** and **Calle dell'Indorador**. *Indorador* is Venetian for 'gilder' and it is common to find Venetian streets named after the trades originally carried out in them.

Corner of Fondamenta degli Eremite and Fondamenta Ognissanti.

Campo Squero.

Calle Lunga San Barnaba.

7 Turn right into **Calle Lunga San Barnaba**. Excellent eateries abound in this short stretch. **Osteria Enoteca San Barnaba** (closed Wed), noted for its exemplary wine list and succulent meat dishes, stands on the corner of Calle Lunga San Barnaba and **Calle delle Turchette**, named after the Ottoman female prisoners brought to Venice in the 15th century with the aim of converting them to Christianity. A little further along is retro clothing store, **Vintage a Go Go** (closed Sun), where you can pick up vintage Pucci and Gucci.

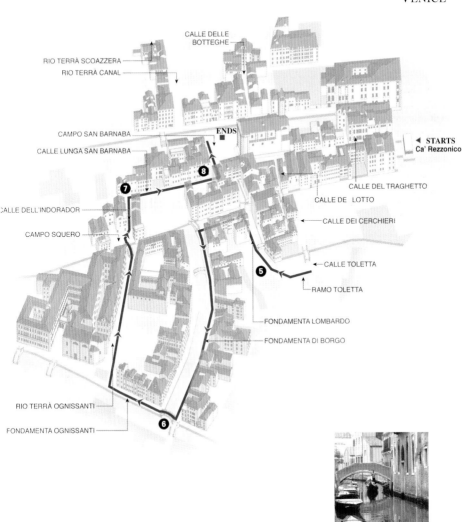

CALLE DELLE BOTTEGHE

RIO TERRÀ SCOAZZERA

RIO TERRÀ CANAL

CAMPO SAN BARNABA

CALLE LUNGA SAN BARNABA

ENDS

◀ STARTS
Ca' Rezzonico

CALLE DELL'INDORADOR

CAMPO SQUERO

CALLE DEL TRAGHETTO

CALLE DE LOTTO

CALLE DEI CERCHIERI

CALLE TOLETTA

RAMO TOLETTA

FONDAMENTA LOMBARDO

FONDAMENTA DI BORGO

RIO TERRÀ OGNISSANTI

FONDAMENTA OGNISSANTI

Rio di San Barnaba.

Floating fruit and vegetable shop by Ponte dei Pugni.

❽ At the end of Calle Lunga San Barnaba is **Campo San Barnaba**. Though the **Church of San Barnaba** holds no treasures, it does have a wonderful brick *campanile* dating back to the 14th century. This *campo* may be small, but it has a tobacconist, a news stand, a restaurant and two great bars. In fact, for the next few stages of the walk, opportunities for alcoholic stop-offs are seemingly endless.

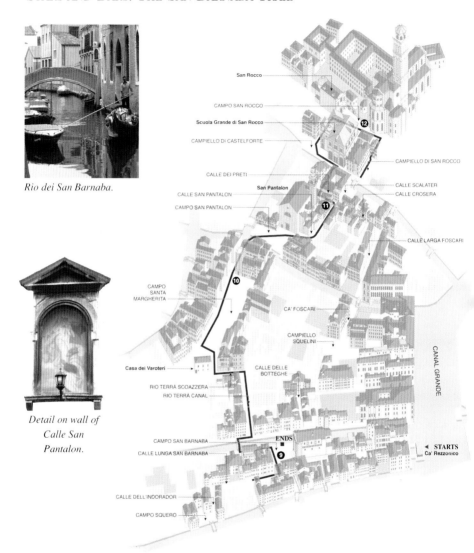

Rio dei San Barnaba.

Detail on wall of Calle San Pantalon.

❾ Turning immediately left out of Calle Lunga, skirt the *campo* and turn left again, past the floating greengrocer's. If you continue down the canal on this side you reach **Fondazione Bevilacqua La Masa** (closed Tues), the *über* cool contemporary art gallery. But your route is across **Ponte dei Pugni**: check out the stone footprints marking where opponents took up their positions for violent fistfights, outlawed in 1705. Going up **Rio terrà Canal**, turn left into **Rio Terrà Scoazzera** and then right to reach **Campo Santa Margherita**, Dorsoduro's largest square. The free-standing house directly in front of you is **Casa dei Varoteri**, with a delicate bas-relief on its façade. As well as any number of pizzerias and bars, this *campo* contains a fine 14thC palace, while its shady park benches allow you to cool off, put your feet up and soak in the atmosphere.

10 Leaving the *campo*, head north over **Rio di Ca' Foscari** into **Campo San Pantalon**. The **Church of San Pantalon** holds breathtaking ceiling paintings by Gian Antonio Fumiani, who purportedly fell to his death from scaffolding while completing the work. To the right of the church is **Calle San Pantalon**, a haven for shoppers, including an exclusive interior design store (**Il Canapè**, closed Sun), a hip clothing and accessories emporium (**3856**, closed weekends) and one of the city's best-loved cake shops (**Tonolo**, closed Mon).

Tonolo cake shop.

11 At Tonolo, turn left on to **Calle dei Preti**. To your left and directly opposite you are two popular late-night haunts: **Café Noir** (closed Sun am) and **Café Blue** (in **Calle fianco di Scuola**). From Café Blue, which serves free wi-fi access with your Guinness, head up the street and cross the bridge. You are now behind the **Scuola Grande di San Rocco**. Take time to admire the charming Campiello di Castelforte and its busy canal junction before following the building around, turning right into **Campo San Rocco**. The **Scuola Grande di San Rocco**, founded as a charitable institution for the sick, houses a sublime cycle of paintings by Venetian master Tintoretto. The sheer number of paintings is awesome, whilst his *Crucifixion* is considered one of Tintoretto's finest works. For more Tintoretto, pop into the adjacent **Church of San Rocco** to see his depictions of the life of Saint Roch.

Frari church from Salizzada di San Rocco.

12 Leave Campo San Rocco, passing the Scuola Grande on your right and turn right. This takes you under an archway into the pretty **Campiello di San Rocco**. Cross **Ponte Scalater** and reach **Calle Crosera**. Directly opposite is **Impronta Café** (closed Sun), a late night bar offering affordable snacks in minimalist surroundings. Going left, at the end of this bustling street is a favourite student hangout, **Bar Caffè Ca' Foscari** (closed Sun). Turning right on to **Calle larga Foscari** you'll see the city's fire station. The fire engine boats, moored under the porticos, are visible from the bridge at the end of the street. On the right, at the foot of the bridge, is **Ca' Foscari**'s faculty of languages where you can sit in the pretty walled garden.

University entrance on CalleDolfin.

Entrance to Ca' Foscari.

⑬ Cross the bridge, and on your left is the entrance to the recently restored **Ca' Foscari**. Now the university's principal building, it was once home to the powerful Foscari family, which produced Doge Francesco Foscari. Henry III of France was wined and dined here in 1574. One of its two wonderful walled courtyards contains an external staircase.

⑭ Leaving Ca' Foscari, turn left into **Campiello Squelini**. This leafy *campo* has three interesting shops: **Arras** (closed Sun) hand weaves fabrics on the large in-store loom, creating accessories and clothes; **L'Angolo del Passato** (closed Sun) has a fine selection of antique glass; the university bookshop **Ca' Foscarina 2** (closed weekends) features books in English.

The huge loom in the Arras clothes shop.

⑮ From the bookshop go down **Calle del Fabbro**. On the left is the **Ca' Macana** workshop, which runs mask-making courses (for info see www.camacana.com). Bearing right, the street runs into **Calle delle Botteghe**, with Ca' Macana's showroom.

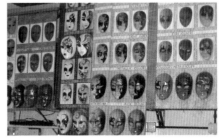

Masks in production at the Ca' Macana workshop.

⑯ At the foot of the bridge taking you back to Campo San Barnaba is the shop (now a mask and gift shop, **Carta Alta**; closed Sun) where Katherine Hepburn met her Italian lover in David Lean's romance *Summertime*. The adjacent canal is where the protagonist literally took the plunge, permanently ruining her eyesight in the process. To the right of the church façade is Calle del Traghetto, where you can visit **Indorador,** Augusto Mazzon's workshop (closed Sun).

Masks on sale outside the Carta Alta gift shop.

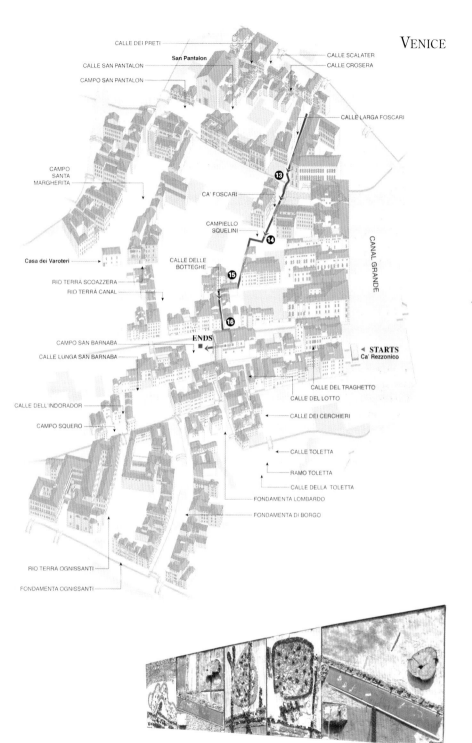

CALLE DEI PRETI

CALLE SCALATER
CALLE CROSERA

San Pantalon

CALLE SAN PANTALON

CAMPO SAN PANTALON

CALLE LARGA FOSCARI

❶❸

CAMPO
SANTA
MARGHERITA

CA' FOSCARI

CAMPIELLO
SQUELINI

❶❹

Casa dei Varoteri

CALLE DELLE
BOTTEGHE

❶❺

RIO TERRÀ SCOAZZERA

RIO TERRÀ CANAL

❶❻

CAMPO SAN BARNABA

ENDS ◄━

CALLE LUNGA SAN BARNABA

◄ STARTS
Ca' Rezzonico

CANAL GRANDE

CALLE DEL TRAGHETTO

CALLE DEL LOTTO

CALLE DELL'INDORADOR

CALLE DEI CERCHIERI

CAMPO SQUERO

CALLE TOLETTA

RAMO TOLETTA

CALLE DELLA TOLETTA

FONDAMENTA LOMBARDO

FONDAMENTA DI BORGO

RIO TERRA OGNISSANTI

FONDAMENTA OGNISSANTI

Collage on wall on Campiello Squelini.

Underneath the Arches: San Polo Circuit

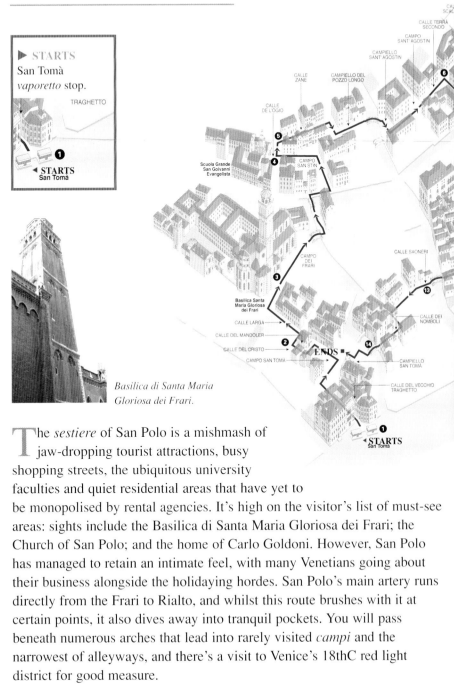

▶ **STARTS**
San Tomà *vaporetto* stop.

TRAGHETTO

①

◀ **STARTS**
San Tomà

Basilica di Santa Maria Gloriosa dei Frari.

The *sestiere* of San Polo is a mishmash of jaw-dropping tourist attractions, busy shopping streets, the ubiquitous university faculties and quiet residential areas that have yet to be monopolised by rental agencies. It's high on the visitor's list of must-see areas: sights include the Basilica di Santa Maria Gloriosa dei Frari; the Church of San Polo; and the home of Carlo Goldoni. However, San Polo has managed to retain an intimate feel, with many Venetians going about their business alongside the holidaying hordes. San Polo's main artery runs directly from the Frari to Rialto, and whilst this route brushes with it at certain points, it also dives away into tranquil pockets. You will pass beneath numerous arches that lead into rarely visited *campi* and the narrowest of alleyways, and there's a visit to Venice's 18thC red light district for good measure.

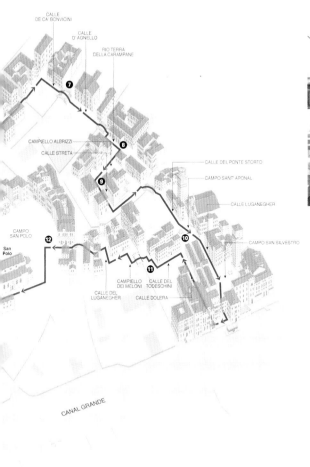

Fondamenta del Banco Salviati.

Scuola Grande San Giovanni Evangelista.

A relief sculpture on Scuola Grande San Giovanni Evangelista.

ENDS
Campo San Tomà.
Nearest *vaporetto*
stop: San Toma.

49

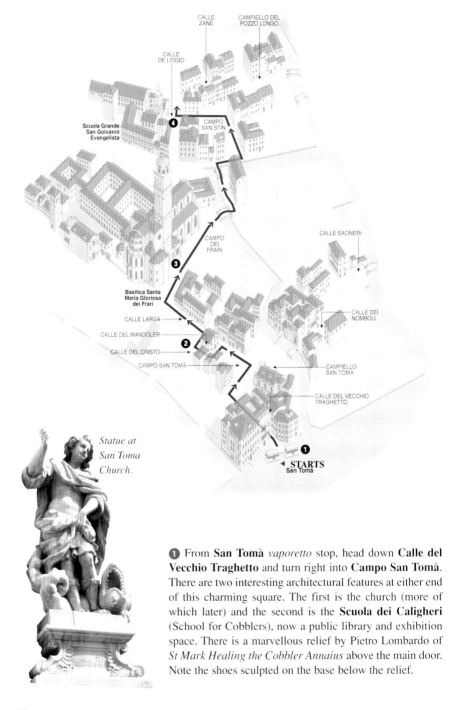

Statue at San Toma Church.

① From **San Tomà** *vaporetto* stop, head down **Calle del Vecchio Traghetto** and turn right into **Campo San Tomà**. There are two interesting architectural features at either end of this charming square. The first is the church (more of which later) and the second is the **Scuola dei Caligheri** (School for Cobblers), now a public library and exhibition space. There is a marvellous relief by Pietro Lombardo of *St Mark Healing the Cobbler Annaius* above the main door. Note the shoes sculpted on the base below the relief.

Basilica Santa Maria Gloriosa dei Frari.

❷ Taking **Calle del Mondoler** to the left of the *Scuola*, passing doll hospital-cum-retro store **Il Baule Blu** (closed Sun), finds you in **Calle del Cristo**. Here is the second of the two fabulous *cioccolaterie* in Venice, **VizioVirtù**, which makes everything from red-hot chilli chocolate to cocoa pasta. Crossing the *calle*, veer right down **Calle Larga** and soaring above you is the Gothic goliath **Basilica Santa Maria Gloriosa dei Frari**. The Franciscans were granted this patch of Venice in the mid 13th century and the present church was built 200 years later. Though relatively unassuming on the outside, this monster houses a host of art treasures. Entering the church, your eyes light upon Titian's wondrous *Assumption* above the main altar. In fact, the Frari boasts two Titians: the *Madonna di Ca' Pesaro*, to the left of the main entrance, is noted for its intimacy and humanity. And there is more. A Donatello sculpture of St John the Baptist and a Bellini masterpiece in the sacristy are not to be missed. From the sacristy, check out the marvellous cloisters.

Fondamenta Contarini.

❸ Emerging from the gloom, to your right is the **Archivio di Stato**, bulging with Venetian documents dating back to the 9th century and thus beloved of historians. Cross the bridge out of the square and turn left. Have a drink in **Caffè dei Frari**, one of Venice's best-loved bars, before moving on the next bridge and into **Campo San Stin**. This square has a local feel, with shops catering for everyday needs.

Courtyard in the entrance of Scuola Grande.

❹ Behind the campo, in **Calle de l'Ogio**, stands the **Scuola Grande San Giovanni Evangelista**. Enter the courtyard under Pietro Lombardo's magnificent screen portal bearing an eagle, symbol of St John the Evangelist. To the right is the *Scuola*, founded in 1261 by a fraternity of flagellants. It houses a double staircase designed by Maurizio Codussi.

5 With your back to the portal, go under the narrow archway in front of you and down **Calle Zane**. Turn right, then left, into **Campiello del Pozzo Longo**. Continue under the **Sotoportego del Pozzo Longo** and cross the bridge into **Campiello Sant'Agostin**. This *campo* flanks a busy canal and is taken up by outdoor seating for **Da Baffo** (closed Sun), a lively bar offering good-value light meals. Continuing north you come to **Campo Sant'Agostin**, which contains a Venetian institution, **Due Colonne Pizzeria** (closed Sun). Further along, on the left side of **Calle Terrà Secondo** is a beautiful relief above a shop entrance, whilst on the right are plaques marking the printing school.

Relief on façade in Calle Terrà Secondo.

Inscription on north-facing façade in Calle Terrà Secondo.

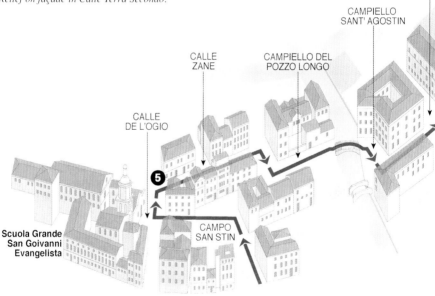

CAMPO SANT' AGO...

CAMPIELLO SANT' AGOSTIN

CALLE ZANE

CAMPIELLO DEL POZZO LONGO

CALLE DE L'OGIO

5

CAMPO SAN STIN

Scuola Grande San Goivanni Evangelista

Rio delle Due Torri.

6 Turning right into **Calle Scaleter** is another Venetian icon: the Michelin-starred **Da Fiore** restaurant (closed Sun and Mon), which now holds cookery classes. With Da Fiore on your right, turn left, cross the bridge and take the second right into **Calle de Ca' Bonvicini**.'Ca' Bonvicini, an erstwhile patrician palace, was once a university faculty building. The family name Bonvicini means 'good neighbours'.

7 Cross the crooked bridge, down **Calle d'Agnello**, arriving at **Ponte delle Tette** (literally 'Tits Bridge'). To dissuade men from acts of sodomy in the final dissolute years of the Serenissima, prostitutes were allowed to bare their wares from this bridge, hoping to pull in the punters passing down the canal. From the bridge, turn right and then left into **Rio Terrà delle Carampane**. Much of this area was a mini ghetto brimming with ladies of the night under strict control of Venetian laws. In place of brothels is an excellent – though not particularly chummy – fish restaurant, **Antiche Carampane** (closed Sun and Mon).

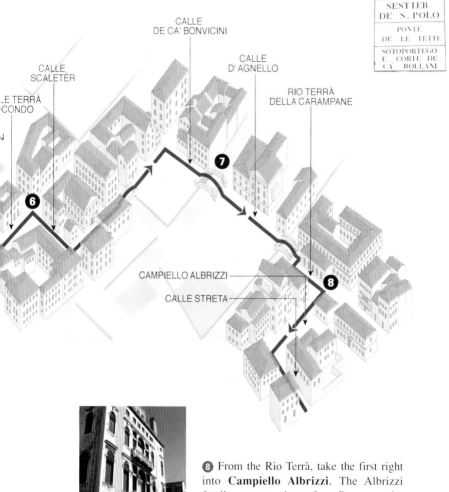

CALLE
DE CA' BONVICINI

CALLE
D' AGNELLO

CALLE
SCALETÈR

RIO TERRÀ
DELLA CARAMPANE

_E TERRÀ
CONDO

6

7

CAMPIELLO ALBRIZZI

CALLE STRETA

8

SESTIER
DE S. POLO

PONTE
DE LE TETTE

SOTOPORTEGO
E CORTE DE
CA BOLLANI

Campiello Albrizzi.

8 From the Rio Terrà, take the first right into **Campiello Albrizzi**. The Albrizzi family were merchants from Bergamo who made their fortune from fabrics and oil and their good name from fighting the Turks. The family still reside in the imposing palace in this little square.

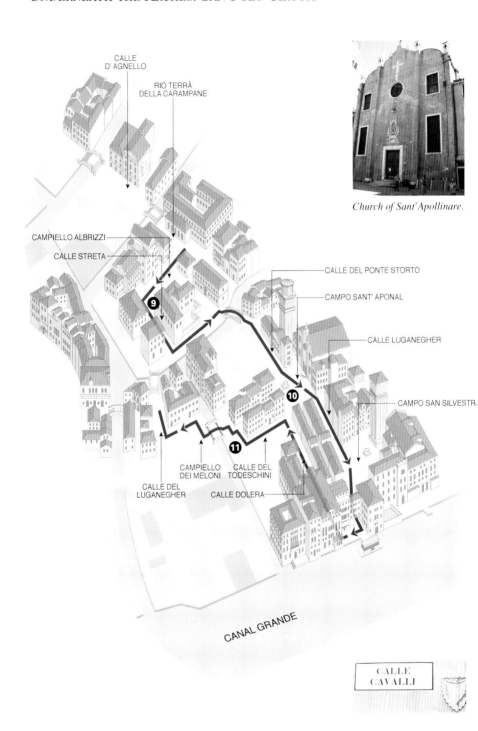

Church of Sant'Apollinare.

CALLE D'AGNELLO

RIO TERRÀ DELLA CARAMPANE

CAMPIELLO ALBRIZZI

CALLE STRETA

CALLE DEL PONTE STORTO

CAMPO SANT'APONAL

9

CALLE LUGANEGHER

10

CAMPO SAN SILVESTR

11

CAMPIELLO DEI MELONI

CALLE DEL TODESCHINI

CALLE DEL LUGANEGHER

CALLE DOLERA

CANAL GRANDE

CALLE CAVALLI

❾ Leaving the square via the aptly-named **Calle Stretta** ('narrow alley'), turn left under the porticoed **Sotoportego Tamossi**, named after the banking dynasty that once lived here, and then pass under **Sotoportego del Banco Salviati**. The stucco-covered **Palazzo Salviati** (no. 1510) is at the end of the *fondamenta*. To the left of **Ponte Storto**, across the *rio*, is **Palazzo Molin-Cappello**, home to Bianca Cappello, who was sentenced to death for running off with a bank clerk in 1563. Cross Ponte Storto and head down **Calle del Ponte Storto** into **Campo Sant'Aponal**. The **Church of Sant'Apollinare** (Sant'Aponal) was first built in the 11th century, though the present edifice is from the 1400s. Note the Veneto-Byzantine *campanile*.

A well in Campiello Barzizza.

❿ Making a diagonal of the *campo*, take **Calle Luganegher** down to **Campo San Silvestro**. This spacious square alongside the church has benches on which to take a breather, but if you need a drink, head for **Altrove** (closed Sun), one of the many new bars that have sprouted up throughout the city. If you take the *sotoportego* from the back of the *campo* to the back of the church, you reach San Silvestro *traghetto* stop, which ferries you to the other side of Rialto. Your route, however, is under the **Sotoportego de la Pasina** (near the San Silvestro *vaporetto* stop). Go through the next archway into **Campiello Barzizza**. This courtyard, with its pink marble well, is named after Palazzo Barzizza, overlooking the Grand Canal.

Inside the shop Il Pavone.

⓫ From here bear right, left and immediately right to reach the bustling **Campiello dei Meloni**. Here, at **Il Pavone** (closed Tues), you can watch artisans creating wonderful marbleised paper products, whilst further along, the famous **Pasticceria Rizzardini** serves a great selection of traditional Venetian cakes. With the patisserie behind you, take **Calle del Luganegher** directly opposite. Turning left, then right, then left again, cross **Ponte Cavalli** to burst into **Campo San Polo**.

⑫ This spacious square once hosted public events, such as bull baiting and masquerades. The square was also the infamous site of Lorenzino de' Medici's murder in 1548. Now Campo San Polo is home to the less dramatic open-air cinema in August and carnival events (including a miniscule ice rink) in winter. In the south-eastern corner stands the **Church of San Polo**, with an exquisite Gothic portal and ferocious Romanesque lions guarding the base of the *campanile*. Inside are 14 paintings by Giandomenico Tiepolo and a haunting *Last Supper* by Tintoretto. Leaving the church, turn right and cross **Ponte di San Polo**. On the bridge is the entrance to **La Patatina**, one of the friendliest *osterie* in town. Stand at the bar for a glass of wine and *cicchetti* (bar snacks) or sit at a table.

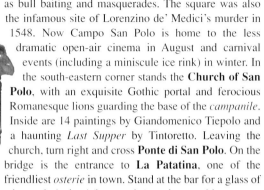

Relief on Church of San Polo.

Archway to Church of San Polo.

Courtyard of Casa Goldoni.

⑬ From La Patatina, continue along the narrow **Calle Saoneri**. You risk getting stuck in a human traffic jam, before turning left on to **Rio terrà dei Nomboli**. From here proceed right to **Calle dei Nomboli**. This street has two points of interest: on the right is **Tragicomica**, an Aladdin's cave of masks, and on the left is the delightful **Casa Goldoni**, home to the Venetian playwright and now a museum and theatre studies library.

On Calle Saoneri.

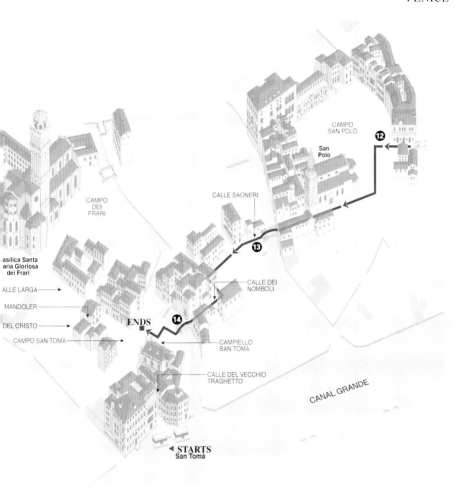

CAMPO
SAN POLO

San
Polo

⑫

CALLE SAONERI

⑬

CAMPO
DEI
FRARI

asilica Santa
aria Gloriosa
dei Frari

CALLE DEI
NOMBOLI

ALLE LARGA

MANDOLER

ENDS   ⑭

DEL CRISTO

CAMPO SAN TOMÀ

CAMPIELLO
SAN TOMA

CALLE DEL VECCHIO
TRAGHETTO

CANAL GRANDE

◄ STARTS
San Tomà

Relief on north side of Sao Tomà church.

⑭ From Casa Goldoni, cross **Ponte San Tomà** into **Campiello San Tomà**. Facing you is the northern side of the Church of San Tomà, with the Gothic relief-lunette of Madonna spreading her protective cape around her followers. If you turn left, you will reach the San Tomà *traghetto* stop, which crosses the Grand Canal to Sant'Angelo. Turning right, you reach Campo San Tomà with its delicate white marble 17thC façade. On the church's right flank is a 14thC fragment of a sarcophagus. And from here you are mere steps away from San Tomà *vaporetto* stop.

Food Walk:
Rialto to San Stae

This walk takes in the neighbourhoods of San Polo and Santa Croce and it offers the standard fare of churches, squares and palaces. However, food is also very much on the menu. From every kind of ingredient laid out in splendour at Rialto market, to traditional Venetian bar snacks, not forgetting a nibble of sushi, this walk is a foodie's dream, serving up hidden *osterie* and bars. Carnivores, veggies and fish-lovers are all looked after.

The route begins at the still-throbbing heart of Venetian commercial life: Rialto market. From here

▶ STARTS
Rialto market.
Nearest *vaporetto* stop:
Rialto Mercato.

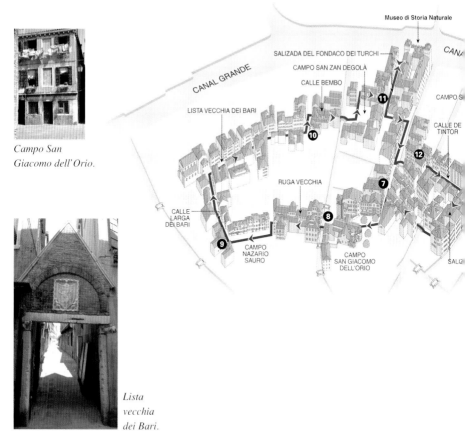

Campo San Giacomo dell'Orio.

Lista vecchia dei Bari.

you go to one of the city's oldest churches, then through back streets (ideal for snacking), to a palace-turned-gallery, pausing at one of Venice's liveliest *campi* before continuing through one of its loveliest and quietest squares. You'll enjoy a Jurassic moment in a Turkish *fonduq* then visit a church-turned-exhibition space.

Vaporetti stop at Rialto Mercato on weekdays, but on Sundays you can start from the Rialto *traghetto* stop, slightly west of the *vaporetto* stop. This route is best done on Tuesday to Saturday mornings, when the fish market is open.

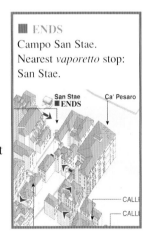

■ ENDS
Campo San Stae.
Nearest *vaporetto* stop:
San Stae.

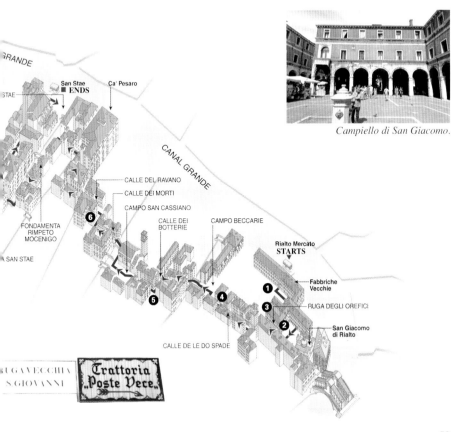

Campiello di San Giacomo.

San Giacomo di Rialto façade.

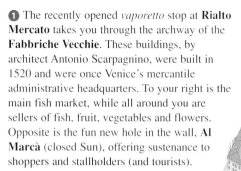

1 The recently opened *vaporetto* stop at **Rialto Mercato** takes you through the archway of the **Fabbriche Vecchie**. These buildings, by architect Antonio Scarpagnino, were built in 1520 and were once Venice's mercantile administrative headquarters. To your right is the main fish market, while all around you are sellers of fish, fruit, vegetables and flowers. Opposite is the fun new hole in the wall, **Al Marcà** (closed Sun), offering sustenance to shoppers and stallholders (and tourists).

San Giacomo di Rialto.

2 Take the archway to the left of the bar. You are now standing before Venice's oldest church: **San Giacomo di Rialto**. Its supposed foundation date, 25th March 421, is that of the city itself, though little remains of the original structure. It still bears the original Greek cross plan and the interior has ancient marble columns on 11thC capitals. Above the Gothic portico is a 24-hour clock. To your right are two wonderful eateries: the first, **Naranzeria**, is a self-consciously hip sushi bar. The second is the more down-to-earth **Bancogiro** (both closed Mon). Each offers open-air dining, intimate upstairs seating or a stand-up drink at the bar.

3 Head up **Ruga degli Orefici**, with the Rialto Bridge behind you. Turning left, you will find the **Church of San Giovanni Elemosinario**. This Renaissance building – often overlooked by jostling tourists – was probably designed by Scarpagnino. It contains a Titian above the altar and a delightful medieval sculptural relief fragment depicting the Nativity. Cross the street, elbowing through the hordes, into **Ruga dei Due Mori**. Directly ahead is **All'Arco** (closed Sun), a favourite stop-off on the way home from market. Great *crostini* (crusty bread with delicious toppings) and *prosecco* that you can enjoy at its outdoor tables. Further up on the right is rival **Cantina Do Mori** (closed Sun), which claims to be the oldest *bacaro* in town, with wonderful wines and snacks, particularly the *francobolli* ('stamps': bite-size sandwiches). For more titbits, just around the corner is **I Storti** (closed Sun) a rough-and-ready *cicchetteria*.

Cantina Do Mori.

LE DEL RAVANO

LE DEI MORTI

MPO SAN CASSIANO

CANAL GRANDE

CALLE DEI BOTTERIE

CAMPO BECCARIE

Rialto Mercato
STARTS

①

④

③

②

Fabbriche Vecchie

RUGA DEGLI OREFICI

San Giacomo di Rialto

CALLE DE LE DO SPADE

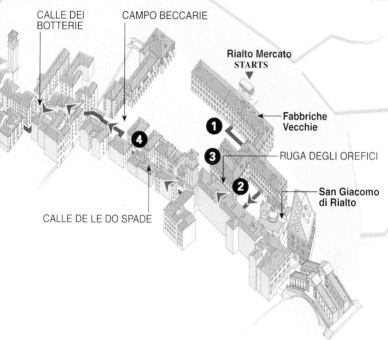

④ Going under the archway ahead takes you to **Calle de le Do Spade** and the *cantina* of the same name (closed Sun) for more Venetian fare. Moving on across the bridge and down the alley, turn left into busy **Calle dei Botteri** (named after the cask makers who had worked in the area from the 13th century). Bull baiting once happened here.

Ruga dei Do Mori.

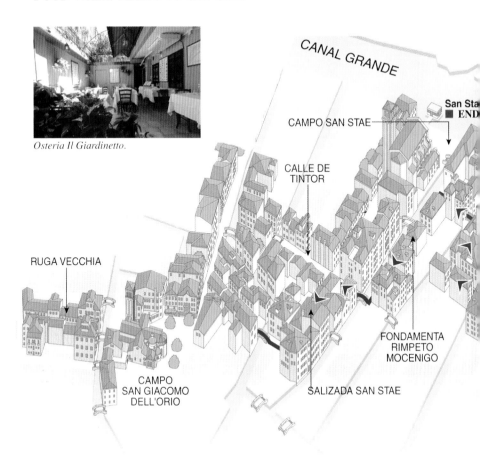

Osteria Il Giardinetto.

❺ Turn right into **Calle dei Cristi** to reach **Campo San Cassiano**. The church houses three Tintorettos and the gruesome *The Martyrdom of St Cassian*, depicting his death at the hands of pen-wielding pupils, an event that made him the patron saint of schoolteachers. From the church, you can pop over the left-hand bridge to **Al Nono Risorto** (closed Wed). Its wisteria-laden garden and great prices make it a popular haunt. Taking the bridge to the far right of the square, enter **Calle dei Morti** ('street of

the dead'), so-called after the cemetery that once adjoined the church. At no. 2252 is a sign stating '*Antica Agenzia Autorizzata Per Operazioni Presso Il Monte Di Pietà*', indicating a charitable loan scheme that functioned like a pawnshop. Despite the 'charitable' nature of these shops, these institutions were rigorous in their debt collection. At the end of the street is **Osteria Antico Giardinetto** (closed Mon), serving delights from the deep on its pretty patio.

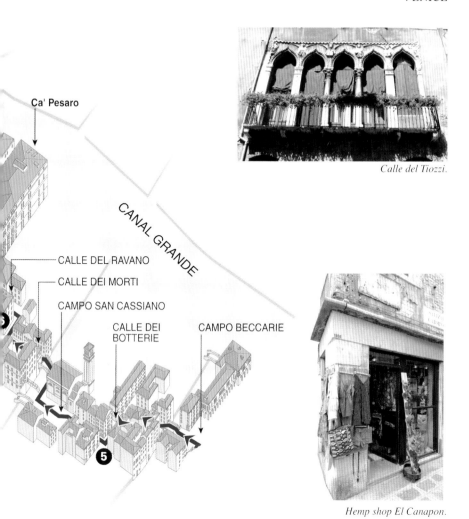

Calle del Tiozzi.

Ca' Pesaro

CANAL GRANDE

CALLE DEL RAVANO
CALLE DEI MORTI
CAMPO SAN CASSIANO
CALLE DEI BOTTERIE
CAMPO BECCARIE

5

Hemp shop El Canapon.

6 Turn right, then left into **Calle del Ravano** and over the bridge into **Calle dei Tiozzi**. Turn right on **Fondamenta di Ca' Pesaro** to **Ca' Pesaro, Galleria d'Arte Moderna**. Once home to the wealthy and powerful Pesaro family, the building designed by Longhena now houses a small modern art collection, including sculptures by Medardo Rosso. Leaving the museum, cross **Ponte Pesaro** and tramp down **Calle Pesaro.** (You can cut short the walk here by turning right to Campo San Stae.) Turn left down the photogenic **Fondamenta Rimpeto Mocenigo**. Turn right over **Ponte de la Rioda** and so down the street, turning left in **Salizada San Stae**. Walking past the hemp clothes shop **El Canapon** (closed Sun) and the state middle school in **Salizzada Carminati**, turn right into **Ramo Carminati** and go straight on.

7 At the end of the alley, turn left into one of Venice's liveliest 'local' squares: **Campo San Giacomo dell'Orio**. Thanks to the proximity of two schools, this square is often teeming with kids in the afternoons. With park benches under shady trees and the Co-op supermarket, it is also a popular haunt for local elderly ladies, not to mention the site's open-air tango lessons on hot summer nights. You'll also find **Il Prosecco** (closed Sun), with superlative wines and excellent eats. Don't forget to visit the charming church, which contains a stunning *Madonna and Four Saints* by Lorenzo Lotto. The main treat, however, is the architecture of the church, with its ship's keel roof, a 6thC flowered capital, and a 13thC *campanile*. To enter the church, go into **Campiello del Piovan**. You can eat pricey pizza at **Al Refolo** (closed Mon) in this picture-perfect spot.

Church in Campo San Giacomo dell'Orio.

Il Prosecco, Campo San Giacomo dell'Orio.

Campiello del Piovan.

8 Taking the bridge to the left into **Ruga Vechia**, go left again into **Ramo Orsetti** and then on to **Campo Nazario Sauro**. This square takes its name from the eponymous Italian nationalist hero who captured an Austrian ship in World War I and sailed it to Venice. Arriving in the city, he pressured Italy to take the Entente side. After carrying out more than 60 missions, Sauro was captured and hanged for treason by the Austrians.

View from Ponte Vecchio.

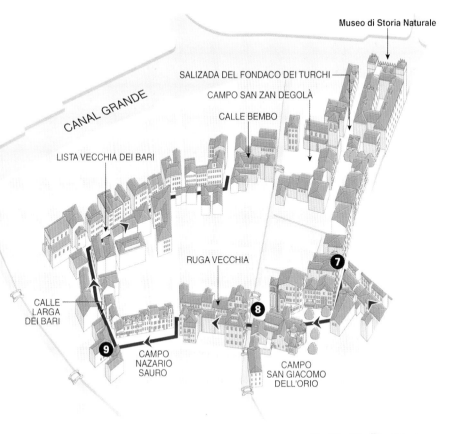

Museo di Storia Naturale

SALIZADA DEL FONDACO DEI TURCHI

CAMPO SAN ZAN DEGOLÀ

CALLE BEMBO

CANAL GRANDE

LISTA VECCHIA DEI BARI

RUGA VECCHIA

CALLE LARGA DEI BARI

CAMPO NAZARIO SAURO

CAMPO SAN GIACOMO DELL'ORIO

Plaque on Campo Nazario Sauro.

Relief on Lista vecchia dei Bari.

❾ Turning right into **Calle Larga dei Bari** are two more foodie treats: the first is **La Ferrata** (closed Mon), offering a garden, pizza and standard Venetian fare; the second is **Alaska**, serving ice-cream ranging from ginger, rocket and orange, to almond. Turning right on to **Lista Vecchia dei Bari** is another secret garden belonging to **All'Anfora** pizzeria, (closed Wed) and another *cicchetteria* (**Osteria Alba Nova**, closed Sun).

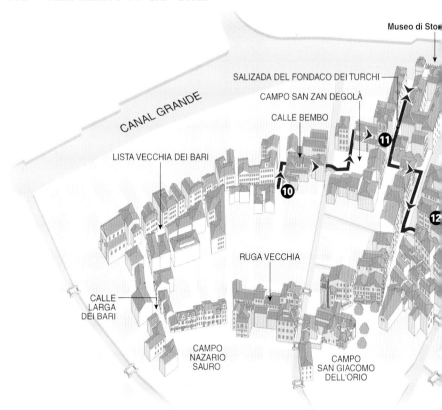

Museo di Sto■

SALIZADA DEL FONDACO DEI TURCHI

CAMPO SAN ZAN DEGOLÀ

CALLE BEMBO

CANAL GRANDE

LISTA VECCHIA DEI BARI

RUGA VECCHIA

CALLE
LARGA
DEI BARI

CAMPO
NAZARIO
SAURO

CAMPO
SAN GIACOMO
DELL'ORIO

10 Heading straight, veering slightly left across **Rio Terrà** and into **Calle Bembo**, will find you in the restful **Campo San Zan Degolà**. The 11thC church of St John the Beheaded is equally soothing on the eye, with both its exterior and interior an homage to simplicity. The interior was recently restored, bringing to light a 14thC fresco.

11 From this haven take **Calle dei Preti** behind the church and then turn left into **Salizzada del Fondaco dei Turchi**. This Venetian-Byzantine building was once rented to Turkish traders, hence its name. It is now the **Museo di Storia Naturale** (closed Mon), boasting an aquarium of

aquatic life from the northern lagoon, and a Dinosaur Room. Note the marble reliefs above the two entrances. Retracing your steps, turn left into **Ramo Secondo del Megio**, then right on to the *fondamenta*, at the end of which is **Ponte del Megio**. Cross the bridge and you'll see **La Zucca** (closed Sun). This canal-side eatery provides an alternative to all things fishy. Vegetarians are well catered for here, and carnivores are respected too, with dishes such as lamb and roast fennel, or ginger pork and rice. Leave room for pudding.

aturale

CANAL GRANDE

San Stae ■ ENDS

Ca' Pesaro

CAMPO SAN STAE

CALLE DE TINTOR

FONDAMENTA RIMPETO MOCENIGO

SALIZADA SAN STAE

Grand Canal from Campo San Stae.

⑫ The last leg of this route takes you partly down **Calle del Megio**, *megio* referring to the grain once stored in what is now an elementary school. Turning left into **Calle del Tintor** and then left back on to **Salizzada San Stae**, to your right is **Palazzo Mocenigo**, previously home to the Mocenigo patrician family that gave the city seven doges, and now a museum of textiles and costumes. On the left is the friendly **Osteria Mocenigo** (closed Mon), offering traditional snacks and meals. At the top of the street is **Campo San Stae** (Sant'Eustachio), its deconsecrated church now an exhibition space used by Switzerland during the Venice Biennale. To the left of the church is a sign referring to the '*Scola dell'arte de Tiraoro e Battioro*', the school for goldbeaters. Opposite the church is San Stae *vaporetto* stop.

Relief on Fondaco dei Turchi.

Grand Canal.

Fresh Air and Simple Pleasures: Ghetto Walk

If you have had enough of Catholic iconography and dark, narrow alleys, then this route offers some respite. After taking in the wealth of churches in southern Venice (walks 1, 3 and 4), you are going north for fresh air and some simple pleasures – a shady stroll, green surroundings, and a picnic lunch you have packed yourself. Yet this route is not all about the great outdoors. While Italian culture has enriched the English language with many significant words, Venice has given it a much less happy one: *ghetto*.

On this walk you will discover the Jewish Ghetto, absorbing its history, eat (if you wish) in its excellent kosher restaurant and pause for thought before the Holocaust memorial in an attractive square. Before you reach the Ghetto, there is a park, a brace of churches and an abattoir. Later comes another church, a swimming pool and a park with its own theatre. The Ghetto museum and synagogues are closed on Saturdays. This is a great route for parents with children – the two parks, the pool and the long, straight streets are easy on the eye and are ideal for kids and carers. Take mosquito repellent if you are intending to spend time in the parks.

CALLE SAN GIOBBE

FONDAMENTA DI CANNAREG

6

5

4

CANALE DI CANNAREGI

CAMPO SAN GIOBBE

PARC SAVORG

▶ STARTS
Ponte delle Guglie
Nearest *vaporetto* stop:
Ponte delle Guglie.

▦ ENDS
Parco Groggia
Nearest *vaporetto* stop:
Sant' Alvise.

Parco Savorgnan.

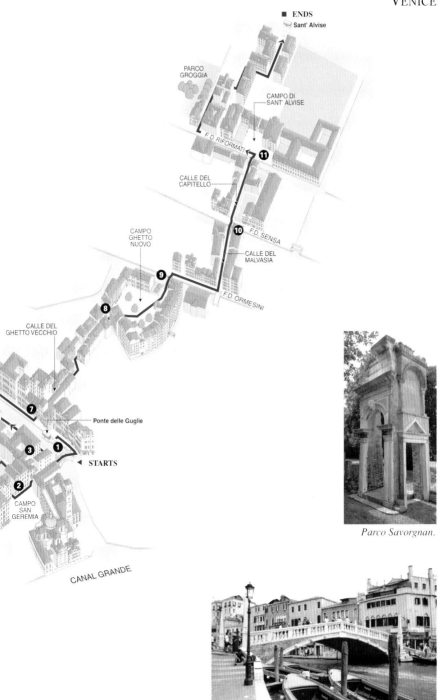

■ ENDS
Sant' Alvise

PARCO
GROGGIA

CAMPO DI
SANT' ALVISE

F. D. RIFORMATI

⓫

CALLE DEL
CAPITELLO

CAMPO
GHETTO
NUOVO

⑩ F.D. SENSA

CALLE DEL
MALVASIA

⑨

F.D. ORMESINI

⑧

CALLE DEL
GHETTO VECCHIO

⑦

Ponte delle Guglie

③ ①

◄ STARTS

②

CAMPO
SAN
GEREMIA

CANAL GRANDE

Parco Savorgnan.

Ponte delle Guglie.

Fresh Air and Simple Pleasures: Ghetto Walk

CALLE
SAN GIOBBE

❶ From the *vaporetto* stop, turn right on to **Ponte delle Guglie** (Bridge of the Obelisks). This bridge is part of Venice's principal artery, swarming with pedestrians going from the railway station towards Rialto. It also spans one of the city's busiest canals, connecting the northern lagoon with the Grand Canal. After crossing the bridge, head down **Salizzada San Geremia** into **Campo San Geremia**. There are two focal points, first, **Palazzo Labia**. Once boasting wealthy merchant owners – it is said that the Labia family ended lavish dinner parties by throwing their gold dishes into the canal, only for servants to dive in and haul them out again. After the fall of the Republic it became a silk factory, later a sawmill. During the Second World War, a munitions carrier exploded and damaged it. Now owned by the RAI (Italian state TV), the *palazzo's* ballroom has frescoes by Tiepolo. The second sight is the **Church of San Geremia**. It is not an especially lovely church, but the chapel of St Lucy is of interest – her relics are stored here.

Parco Savorgnan.

CAMPO
SAN GIOBBE

❷ From the *campo*, go down **Calle Vergola** into **Parco Savorgnan**. Public parks are a rarity in Venice, though the city contains many private gardens concealed behind high walls. The park stands behind **Palazzo Savorgnan**, whose owners filled it with statues and citrus trees. Containing a children's play park, it also has quieter areas ideal for picnics, reading and naps.

San Geremia.

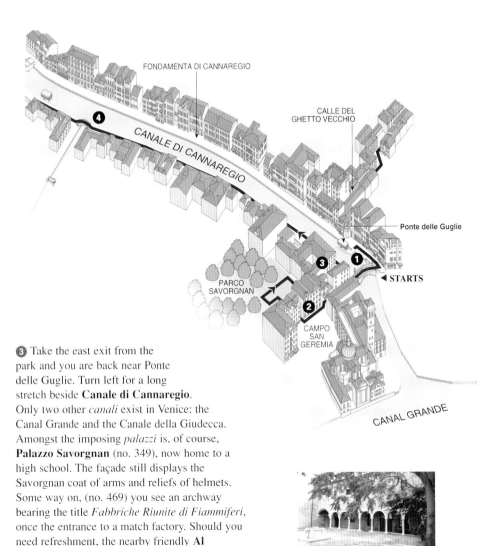

3 Take the east exit from the park and you are back near Ponte delle Guglie. Turn left for a long stretch beside **Canale di Cannaregio**. Only two other *canali* exist in Venice: the Canal Grande and the Canale della Giudecca. Amongst the imposing *palazzi* is, of course, **Palazzo Savorgnan** (no. 349), now home to a high school. The façade still displays the Savorgnan coat of arms and reliefs of helmets. Some way on, (no. 469) you see an archway bearing the title *Fabbriche Riunite di Fiammiferi*, once the entrance to a match factory. Should you need refreshment, the nearby friendly **Al Parlamento** bar is open daily.

Cloisters at San Giobbe.

4 Just ahead is **Ponte della Crea**. The name probably derives from the *creta* (clay) brought to the area for brick making. The pretty canal that this bridge spans had been filled in for centuries, but was reopened in the 1990s. Continuing alongside Canale di Cannaregio, turn left for a detour along **Calle San Giobbe** to reach the church with the same name. Built in 1463, this was Pietro Lombardo's first Venetian commission, and he was responsible for the three statues now housed in the sacristy. Altarpieces by Giovanni Bellini and Carpaccio have been moved to the Accademia galleries, but works by Savoldo and Vivarini remain. Outside the church you can view the cloisters, though unfortunately they are not open to the public.

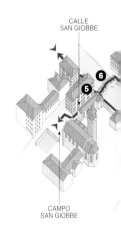

CALLE
SAN GIOBBE

CAMPO
SAN GIOBBE

San Giobbe.

5 Returning to the *fondamenta*, turn left, crossing **Ponte de la Saponela**, to take a detour to one of Venice's best-kept culinary secrets, **Dalla Marisa** (open daily for lunch and Tue, Thur-Sat for dinner). Vegetarians may not like the menu, which offers everything from tripe to pheasant, but the owner, Marisa, comes from butcher's stock. No wonder, given that her restaurant is just a few hundred metres from the former abattoir (further up the *fondamenta*; now a university complex).

6 Turning back, cross **Ponte dei Tre Archi**, the only three-arch bridge in town, to meander back along **Fondamenta di Cannaregio**. Buildings on this side include **Santa Maria delle Penitenti** (no. 893), once a sanctuary for fallen women, and **Palazzo Nani**, a Renaissance family home (no. 1105). A few steps along is **Casa Mattiazzi** (closed Wed pm), a Venetian vintner with a wide range of stock, from cheap table wine to bottles of bubbly.

Ponte dei Tre Archi.

A sure sign that you are approaching the entrance to the Ghetto is **Gam-Gam** (closed Fri eve and Sat), Venice's finest kosher bar and restaurant. You can buy takeaway falafel.

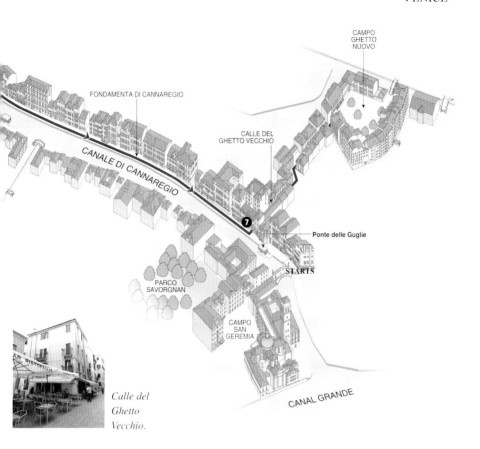

Calle del Ghetto Vecchio.

Relief detail on the Calle del Ghetto Vecchio.

7 To the right of Gam-Gam, duck under the entrance to the Ghetto. In 1516, the *Serenissima* decreed that Jews were permitted to reside in Venice (on the island that once contained the foundry, or Ghetto), though with limitations. Only allowed to be textile traders, moneylenders and doctors, the Jews were locked in at night and, when beyond the Ghetto confines, men were required to show yellow badges and women to wear yellow scarves. In **Calle del Ghetto Vecchio** is a plaque cataloguing the strict Venetian laws governing the Jews, with particularly stern warnings to converted Jews that they must not return to the Ghetto. Confusingly, Ghetto Vecchio is the newer extension of the original Ghetto. Here you find the Spanish and Levantine synagogues. Further along the street is children's bookshop **Laboratorio Blu** (closed Sun) with a range of books in English, and, at the foot of the bridge, is **Chabad**, a site of learning for *yeshiva* students.

❽ Cross the bridge and you are in the heart of the **Ghetto Nuovo**, the Jews' first home in Venice and originally populated by German Ashkenazim Jews. The Sephardim from Spain and Portugal, and the Levantine Jews from the Ottoman Empire, all fleeing persecution, would follow. At its peak, numbers in the Ghetto reached 4,000-5,000, hence the high-rise, low-ceilinged housing. In the square is the **Museo Ebraico** (closed Sat), which organizes tours of the synagogues. There is also Arbit Blatas's monument to the Holocaust. During the Second World War, 289 Venetian Jews were

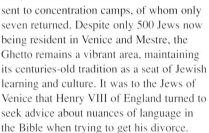

Church of Sant' Alvise.

sent to concentration camps, of whom only seven returned. Despite only 500 Jews now being resident in Venice and Mestre, the Ghetto remains a vibrant area, maintaining its centuries-old tradition as a seat of Jewish learning and culture. It was to the Jews of Venice that Henry VIII of England turned to seek advice about nuances of language in the Bible when trying to get his divorce.

❾ Heading north over the wrought-iron bridge takes you to the attractive **Fondamenta degli Ormesini**. *Ormesini* refers to the silk cloth (originally from the city of Ormus in Asia) produced in this neighbourhood. Keep right until you reach **Calle della Malvasia**. There are many streets of this name throughout the city and they denote areas selling imported wine, particularly the sweet wine called Malvasia, from Monemvasia in Greece. Cross **Ponte della Malvasia** and you are on yet another charming canal-side, **Fondamenta della Sensa**. At the bottom of the bridge is **Ai 40 Ladroni** (closed Mon), serving reasonably priced Venetian food next to a pretty and petite Gothic palace.

❿ Go north along **Calle del Capitello** and cross **Ponte Sant'Alvise** to **Campo Sant'Alvise**. This part of town contains welfare housing and has a strong sense of community, with the **Church of Sant'Alvise** and its adjacent square a meeting place for locals who gather to pass the time of day. With a simple Gothic façade and an interior adorned with 17thC *trompe l'oeil* effects, this parish church is well worth a visit. It houses two Tiepolos on the right-hand wall and a hanging choir with gratings, set aside for the nuns from the neighbouring convent.

⓫ Leaving the church, walk along **Fondamenta dei Riformati** (named after the Reformed Franciscans from the nearby monastery) until reaching another **Calle del Capitello** where you find the entrance to **Parco Groggia**, home to **Teatrino Groggia** (www.comune.venezia.it/teatrinogroggia) and the local swimming pool (its entrance is further along the street). This indoor pool has slightly Byzantine opening hours, and flip-flops and swimming hats are required. But it's a great spot: on clear days you can see the Dolomites shimmering in the distance as you swim. The recently

Bridge from Ghetto to Fondamenta degli Ormesini.

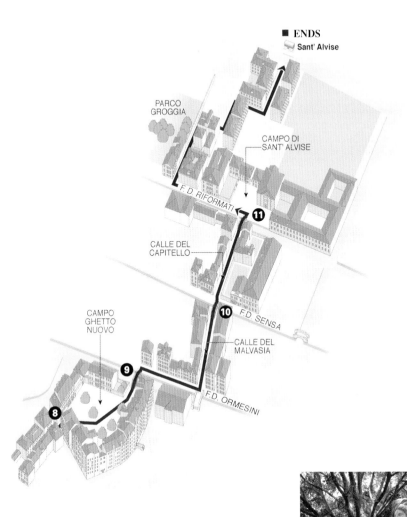

revamped park is an excellent site
for chilling out after a long walk,
whilst the theatre offers music,
experimental theatre, workshops and
special performances for children.
From here, it is a short walk to
Sant'Alvise boat stop.

Parco Groggia.

75

Heart of Cannaregio: from San Marcuola to Ca' d'Oro

This linear walk runs through the heart of Cannaregio, crossing its heaving 'main road', Strada Nova. With its glass shops and street vendors, supermarkets and boutiques, this is one of the busiest hubs in Venice. Your walk, however, generally avoids the commercial hotspots, insinuating you into some of the least populous pockets of the city. A cornucopia of churches and Tintoretto masterpieces is in store, ranging from the pint-sized charm of San Felice to the grand magnificence of Madonna dell'Orto and the distinctly odd Santa Maddalena. The walk starts with a humdrum church but ends with the glorious Gothic Ca' d'Oro. There are also opportunities for gambling, eating and drinking: you'll pass a casino, and a pretty stretch of *fondamenta* groaning with restaurants.

Campo de l'Abbazia.

STARTS ▶ ❶
San Marcuola

▶ STARTS
San Marcuola.
Nearest *vaporetto* stop:
San Marcuola.

Fondamenta Gasparo Contarini.

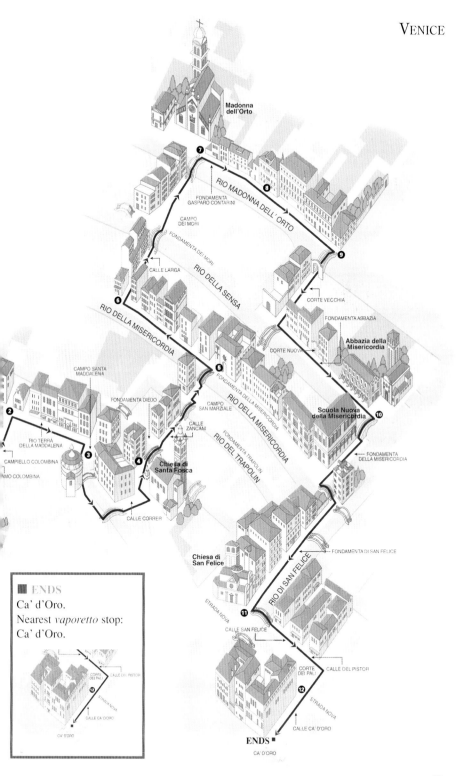

Madonna dell'Orto

7

RIO MADONNA DELL' ORTO

8

FONDAMENTA GASPARO CONTARINI

CAMPO DEI MORI

FONDAMENTA DEI MORI

9

CALLE LARGA

6

RIO DELLA SENSA

CORTE VECCHIA

RIO DELLA MISERICORDIA

FONDAMENTA ABBAZIA

CAMPO SANTA MADDALENA

FONDAMENTA DIEDO

5

FONDAMENTA DELLA MISERICORDIA

CORTE NUOVA

Abbazia della Misericordia

2

RIO TERRA DELLA MADDALENA

CAMPO SAN MARZIALE

CALLE ZANCANI

RIO DELLA MISERICORDIA

FONDAMENTA TRAPOLIN

Scuola Nuova della Misericordia

10

CAMPIELLO COLOMBINA

3

4

RIO DEL TRAPOLIN

FONDAMENTA DELLA MISERICORDIA

MO COLOMBINA

Chiesa di Santa Fosca

CALLE CORRER

Chiesa di San Felice

FONDAMENTA DI SAN FELICE

STRADA NOVA

RIO DI SAN FELICE

11

CALLE SAN FELICE

CORTE DEI PALI

CALLE DEL PISTOR

12

STRADA NOVA

CALLE CA' D'ORO

ENDS

CA' D'ORO

Plaque commemorating
Richard Wagner.

1 Hop off the *vaporetto* and you find yourself standing before the unfinished brick façade of **San Marcuola**. No saint of this name exists: it is an amalgamation of Saints Ermagora and Fortunato. The unprepossessing church contains one of Tintoretto's earlier renditions of *The Last Supper*, as well as statues by Gianmaria Morleiter. Leaving the square, turn right to cross **Ponte Storto** down on to the pretty *fondamenta*. From here turn right into **Ramo Colombina** and **Campiello Colombina**. The square is not named after the *commedia dell'arte* character, but a family of shop owners. Isabel and Cristina de la Colombina were registered as living in this neighbourhood in 1582. The next square is **Campiello Vendramin**, the back entrance to **Palazzo Vendramin Calergi**, designed by Mauro Codussi in the early 1500s. Both the Grand Canal and *campiello* palace walls bear memorials to Wagner, who died here in 1883. The *palazzo* now houses the Casinò.

Church of San Marcuola.

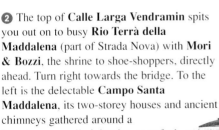

Ponte Storto.

2 The top of **Calle Larga Vendramin** spits you out on to busy **Rio Terrà della Maddalena** (part of Strada Nova) with **Mori & Bozzi**, the shrine to shoe-shoppers, directly ahead. Turn right towards the bridge. To the left is the delectable **Campo Santa Maddalena**, its two-storey houses and ancient chimneys gathered around a Renaissance well giving it a cosy feel. The circular church, inspired by the Pantheon in Rome, has an eye in a triangle and circle on the façade, and a tabernacle with marble reliefs on the back.

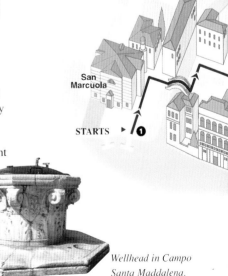

Wellhead in Campo
Santa Maddalena.

❸ Heading now briefly back towards the Grand Canal takes you under the attractive **Sotoportego de le Colonete** and down the *fondamenta* of the same name. Cross the bridge and go down **Calle Correr**. The Correr family (of Museo Correr fame) were one of Venice's most illustrious and pious families, producing a Patriarch of Constantinople (in the 13th century), a Pope (15th century) and a Patriarch of Venice (18th century). This narrow alley leads you back on to Strada Nova where you are faced with the pink side of the **Chiesa di Santa Fosca**. Its works of art include *The Holy Family with Donor* by Tintoretto. In the *campo* is a monument to Paolo Sarpi, adviser to the Venetian Republic during the Papal Interdict troubles at the turn of the 17th century. He survived an assassination attempt on the nearby bridge of Santa Fosca.

Sotoportego de le Colonete.

Campo Santa Fosca.

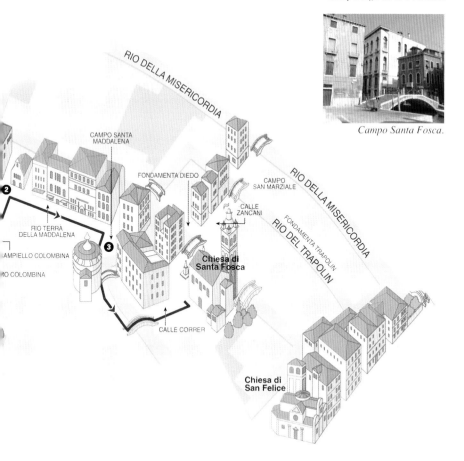

4 At the foot of the bridge on **Fondamenta Diedo** is the popular **Il Santo Bevitore** (closed Sun), with live jazz on Monday nights. Continuing up **Calle Zancani** (at no. 2424) you reach the intriguing *atelier* of local artist Roberto Colussi, famous for his Pinocchio reinventions. Across **Ponte Zancani** is **Campo San Marziale**. The church was originally erected in the 12th century and its chancel was once decorated with works by Tintoretto, which have now disappeared. The wonderful ceiling paintings by Stefano Ricci still remain.

5 Crossing **Ponte della Misericordia** you come to **Fondamenta della Misericordia**, home to many eateries offering something for all palates. First you come to **Iguana** (closed Mon), a lively Mexican restaurant. Next is **Diana** (closed Mon), once a Syrian restaurant, now serving Venetian fare. A little further along is one of Venice's most famous and enduring pub-bars: **Paradiso Perduto** (closed Mon). Once a hang-out for revolutionary students in the 1970s, this ever-popular haunt has refectory tables at which tourists rub shoulders with Venetian youth for cheap eats and live music. Last, and by no means least, is **Da Rioba** (closed Mon), offering traditional Venetian dishes with a contemporary twist.

Fondamenta della Misericordia.

6 From here, turn right into **Calle Larga**, with the pea-green shrine to St Francis. You can also visit Dante Baron's *atelier*. This Venetian-born sculptor creates pieces from driftwood, fragments of Roman earthenware and even burnt timber rescued from La Fenice. On the other side of the bridge are **Fondamenta** and **Campo dei Mori**. Named after the decidedly Moorish-looking statues, they actually represent three Greek traders: Rioba (from whom the aforementioned restaurant takes its name); and Sandi and Afani Mastelli who came from Morea (now the Peloponnese) to set up shop near here. It is also possible that the area was once home to an Islamic merchant community. Along the *fondamenta* (at no.3399) is a plaque testifying that Tintoretto once lived here.

NE PRAETEREAS VIATOR
JAC. ROBUSTI QUI TINTORETTO
DOMUM VETUSTAM
INDE TABULAE INNUMERAE
MENTE PENICILLO IPSIUS PERACRI
AFFABRE ELABORATAE
PUBLICE PRIVATIMQ ASPECTABILES
LATE PRODIERUNT
HOC TE RESCIRE JUVABIT
CURA PRAESENTIS DOMINI
MDCCCXLII

RENOVATA AERE CIVICO 1881

Plaque to Tintoretto o side of his house.

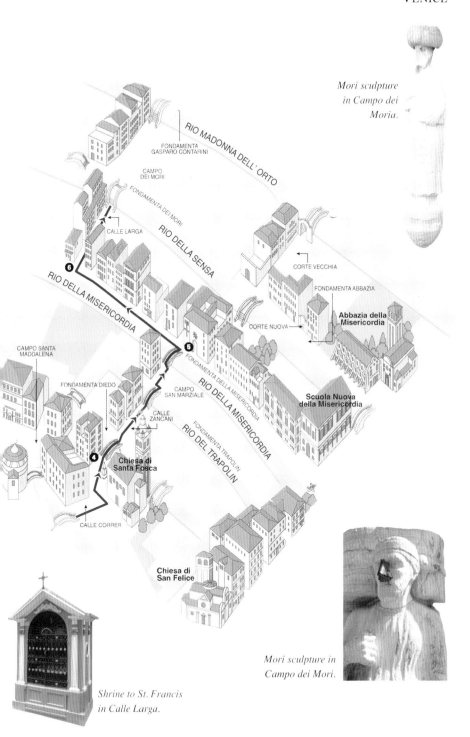

Mori sculpture
in Campo dei
Moria.

RIO MADONNA DELL' ORTO

FONDAMENTA
GASPARO CONTARINI

CAMPO
DEI MORI

FONDAMENTA DEI MORI

CALLE LARGA

RIO DELLA SENSA

CORTE VECCHIA

FONDAMENTA ABBAZIA

❻

RIO DELLA MISERICORDIA

Abbazia della
Misericordia

CAMPO SANTA
MADDALENA

CORTE NUOVA

❺

FONDAMENTA DIEDO

FONDAMENTA DELLA MISERICORDIA

CAMPO
SAN MARZIALE

RIO DELLA MISERICORDIA

Scuola Nuova
della Misericordia

CALLE
ZANCANI

FONDAMENTA TRAPOLIN

❹

RIO DEL TRAPOLIN

Chiesa di
Santa Fosca

CALLE CORRER

Chiesa di
San Felice

Shrine to St. Francis
in Calle Larga.

Mori sculpture in
Campo dei Mori.

81

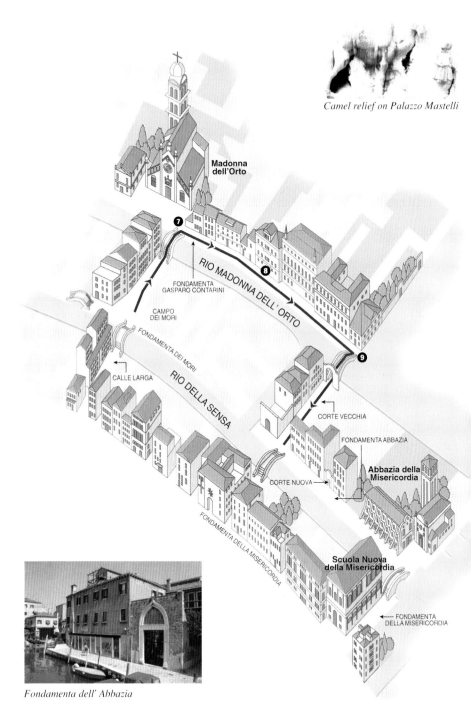

Camel relief on Palazzo Mastelli

Madonna dell'Orto

7

RIO MADONNA DELL'ORTO

8

FONDAMENTA
GASPARO CONTARINI

CAMPO
DEI MORI

FONDAMENTA DEI MORI

CALLE LARGA

RIO DELLA SENSA

9

CORTE VECCHIA

FONDAMENTA ABBAZIA

Abbazia della Misericordia

CORTE NUOVA

FONDAMENTA DELLA MISERICORDIA

Scuola Nuova della Misericordia

FONDAMENTA
DELLA MISERICORDIA

Fondamenta dell' Abbazia

7 Heading north out of the funnel-shaped square and over the bridge takes you to the breathtaking Gothic **Madonna dell'Orto**, otherwise known as the 'Tintoretto church'. Originally dedicated to Saint Christopher, patron saint of gondoliers, the church took its present name in 1377 when a supposedly miraculous statue of the Madonna and Child was brought here (it can be seen in the San Mauro chapel). There are ten works by Tintoretto, including the immense *The Israelites at Mount Sinai* and the *Presentation of the Virgin in the Temple*. Other gems include Titian's *The Archangel Raphael and Tobias* (filched from the church at San Marziale) and Cima da Conegliano's *Saints John the Baptist, Mark, Jerome and Paul*. Tintoretto and his family are buried in the chapel to the right of the high altar.

Madonna dell'Orto.

8 Behind the church is a *vaporetto* stop, but you now walk along the wide expanse of **Fondamenta Gasparo Contarini**, named after the 16thC diplomat and cardinal. To the right of the canal, look out for the 15thC **Palazzo Mastelli**, with its relief of a turbaned man and camel, continuing the Arabic theme of this route. At the furthest point of the *fondamenta* you get a panoramic view of a marina with the islands of Murano and San Michele in the distance.

Fondamenta Gasparo Contarini.

9 Over **Ponte della Saca** and down **Corte Vechia** is another broad stretch of canal side: **Fondamenta Abbazia**. To the right is a charming boatyard (with statues by Dante Baron in the garden). Heading left, you pass **Corte Nuova**, which originally contained dwellings for the poor brothers of the adjacent abbey and is reached through the Gothic doorway with a marble triptych. Take a peep through the iron-grille entrance to view the vast abbey garden before passing under the **Sotoportego de l'Abbazia** to the herringbone square of the **Abbazia della Misericordia**, which contains the two façades of the abbey and the **Scuola Vecchia**.

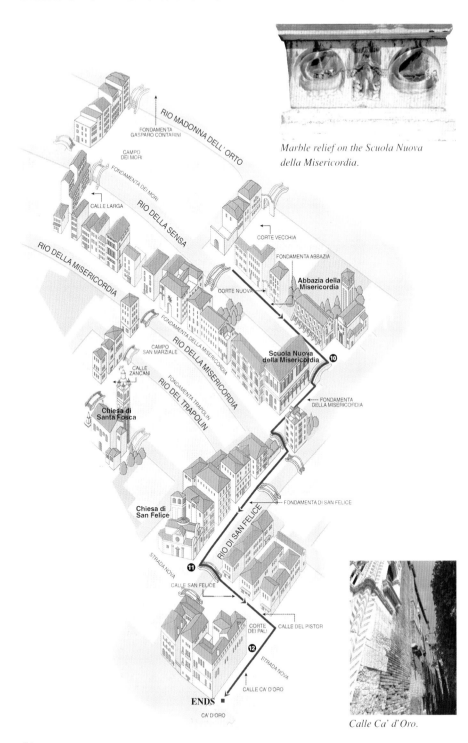

Marble relief on the Scuola Nuova della Misericordia.

Calle Ca' d'Oro.

Fondamenta di San Felice.

10 After crossing **Ponte de l'Abbazia** you go down **Fondamenta della Misericordia,** and past the **Scuola Nuova della Misericordia**. Built by Sansovino, the towering façade was never completed. Cross the bridge to the left and go down pretty **Ramo della Misericordia**. Facing you is the only bridge with no parapet in Venice (though once all bridges were like this). Turning right you are in **Fondamenta di San Felice**, yet another photogenic canal. Just before the church is the fabulous fish restaurant **Vini da Gigio** (closed Mon) serving Venetian specialities with interesting wines. Towards the end of the street is the **Chiesa di San Felice**, founded in the 10th century and housing an altarpiece by Tintoretto.

Corte dei Pali.

11 Over **Ponte Ubaldo Belli** and down **Calle San Felice** brings you to **Corte dei Pali**, home of the spit-and-sawdust **Osteria Ai Osti** (closed Sun), much beloved of local workmen, serving first-rate bar snacks. The Irish Pub is also here. From the *corte* and down **Calle del Pistor** is the deservedly famous **Trattoria Ca' d'Oro** (also known as **Alla Vedova**; closed Thur). The interior is intimate and old-fashioned, with dark wooden tables where local dishes are served. But the best way to enjoy this bistro is at the bar, where there is a wonderful array of *cicchetti*, including the best meatballs in town.

12 From the restaurant go straight ahead, crossing Strada Nova yet again, down **Calle Ca' d'Oro** to **Ca' d'Oro** itself. Still considered by many to be the loveliest palace on the Grand Canal, in its glory days the Venetian Gothic façade with delicate tracery was pale blue and burgundy (not unlike Aston Villa's colours) with gold leaf. Built between 1421 and 1431 for merchant Marino Contarini, it still contains the original staircase and a well head by Bartolomeo Bon in the courtyard. Unfortunately, little else remains of the original interior, which now houses the Giorgio Franchetti Collection. Highlights include a superb *St. Sebastian* by Mantegna (his last work), and *The Annunciation* by Carpaccio. Well worth a visit. The *vaporetto* stop is just to the right of the *palazzo*.

Miracle Church: Gesuiti to Santi Giovanni e Paolo

Miracoli Church.

On the face of it, this walk could seem a little melancholy. The start and the finish offer views of the cemetery island of San Michele; you pass the hospital and a geriatric home; and there's a dearth of shops and eateries. However, don't have second thoughts: this is the route on which you discover one of the jewels in Venice's crown, the magnificent Miracoli church. On either side of this small but astounding building are two other churches, each very different in terms of age and style: the white marble Baroque Gesuiti and the red brick Gothic Santi Giovanni e Paolo.

As a matter of fact, not even the general hospital is an architectural let-down. You are in Venice, after all. Housed in the Scuola Grande di San Marco, it not only possesses one of the loveliest façades in the city, but there's many a treat inside.

Rio dei Mendicanti.

Though restaurants are few, the route will introduce you to some of the finest in Venice and the best hidden.

> ▶ STARTS
> Fondamenta Nuove.
> Nearest *vaporetto* stop:
> Fondamenta Nuove.
>
> ■ ENDS
> Fondamenta Nuove.
> Nearest *vaporetto* stop:
> Ospedale.

Ponte de l'Acquavita.

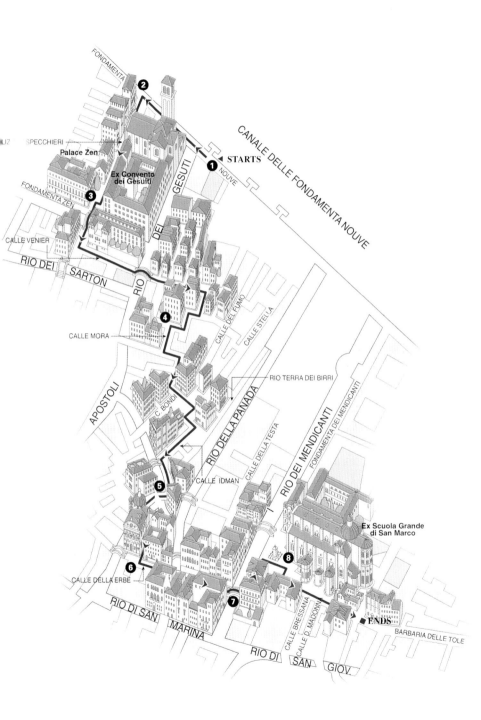

Miracle Church: Gesuiti to Santi Giovanni e Paolo

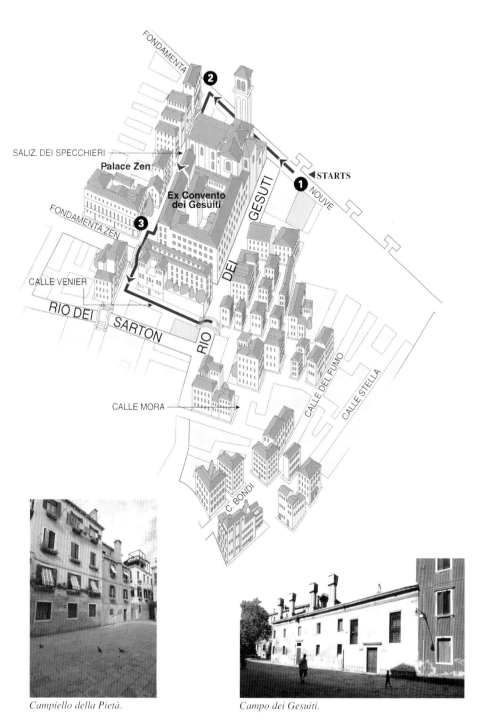

Campiello della Pietà.

Campo dei Gesuiti.

❶ Stepping off the *vaporetto* you find yourself on the long stretch of the **Fondamenta Nuove** overlooking the cemetery island of San Michele. Because it's close to the graveyard, there are many tomb makers and engravers. To avoid dark thoughts, see if (on a clear day) you can make out the Dolomites to the north. The large number of boats stopping here makes it a lively hub, with ACTV employees filling the local bars and cafés. One of these is **Algiubagiò** (closed Tue), serving faultless snacks and meals in a bare-brick, open-beamed interior. From here, turn left, cross **Ponte Donà** and turn left into **Salizada dei Spechieri**.

❷ Spechieri runs into **Campo dei Gesuiti**, a peaceful square with two focal points. The first is the church. Santa Maria Assunta goes by its nickname, **Gesuiti**, from the Jesuits for whom it was built at the beginning of the 18th century. Though disliked in Venice for their links to the papacy, the Jesuits were finally awarded this remote piece of land after 50 years of being refused entry to the city. The clean, white Baroque exterior belies the extravagance of the interior. Its feast of gold leaf and green and white marble, much of it sculpted to look like drapery, takes your breath away (as a gasp of either horror or delight, depending on your taste). Hanging above the first altar on the left is Titian's *The Martyrdom of St Lawrence*, considered one of the first successful nocturnes.

Further along on the right is the **Oratorio dei Crociferi**. Founded in the 13th century, its name derives from the crusaders it once harboured when it was a hospital. The chapel reopened in the 1980s after extensive restoration work.

View of San Michele from Fondamenta Nuove.

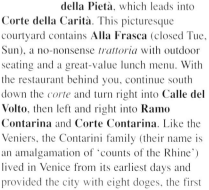
Campo dei Gesuiti.

❸ Across the **Ponte dei Gesuiti**, on your left, is the **Trattoria Storica**. As its name suggests, this restaurant serves age-old Venetian favourites, without fancy contemporary twists. Turning left after the restaurant takes you into **Calle Venier**. The Venier dynasty, one of the founding families of Venice, produced doges, archbishops and admirals, hence the many streets named after them. The next jumble of streets takes you on a labyrinthine route through quiet courtyards and charming *campielli*: cross **Ponte de l'Acquavita** (probably named after the 18thC local liquor store that once stood here) and down the street to **Campiello della Pietà**, which leads into **Corte della Carità**. This picturesque courtyard contains **Alla Frasca** (closed Tue, Sun), a no-nonsense *trattoria* with outdoor seating and a great-value lunch menu. With the restaurant behind you, continue south down the *corte* and turn right into **Calle del Volto**, then left and right into **Ramo Contarina** and **Corte Contarina**. Like the Veniers, the Contarini family (their name is an amalgamation of 'counts of the Rhine') lived in Venice from its earliest days and provided the city with eight doges, the first elected in 1043.

4 From here, go down **Calle More** into the charming **Campiello della Madonna**. This pretty square was once home to the great landscape artist Francesco Guardi, whose vast output includes a view of *The Lagoon Towards Murano from the Fondamenta Nuove* (now at the Fitzwilliam Museum, Cambridge). Leaving the square, take **Calle Moradi**, turn left into **Calle Varisco** and

Campiello Madonna.

keep going until you come to **Campiello Stella** after passing under **Sotoportego Algarotti**. Head south into **Campiello Widmann**, where you will see **Ostaria Boccadoro** (closed Mon), a superb fish restaurant with outdoor tables for open-air dining. Down the long narrow alley to the right of Boccadoro is **Palazzo Widmann**. Originally designed for the Saviotti family by Longhena, it was bought by the rich noble merchant family from Carinthia (Istria), who filled it with treasures. The *palazzo* overlooks a quiet canal, down which you now walk, ducking below **Sotoportego Widmann** and the wonderful arches of **Sotoportego del Magazen**. In Venetian dialect,

Ponte Santa Maria Nuova.

magazen once referred to the vintner-pawnbrokers who accepted personal goods in exchange for cash and low-quality wine.

5 Crossing **Ponte del Piovan** and following the canal, you come to the edge of **Campo Santa Maria Nova** to your right. Here you find an especially fine paper goods shop, **Paolo Olbi**. He began in the 1960s as a bookbinder before crafting stationery from leather and marbled Venetian paper. The square also has a bookstore, a bar, a restaurant, and park benches. Turn left over **Ponte Santa Maria Nova** and you come to **Campiello dei Miracoli** and the pint-sized **Santa Maria dei Miracoli**. Considered one of the most wondrous churches in the world, and often likened to a jewel box, it was built in the 1480s by Pietro Lombardo and his sons to house a supposedly miraculous Madonna painting. This image was believed to have resuscitated a man who had been underwater in the Giudecca Canal for 30 minutes and to have erased all traces of a knife attack from a woman's body. Multi-coloured marble – left over from the Basilica of St Mark's – covers the building from its pilasters and cornices of dark stone to the false *loggia* and crowning lunette. The interior is equally colourful and ornate, with Lombardo's carvings covering the columns and balustrades. The 50 ceiling paintings are by Pennacchi.

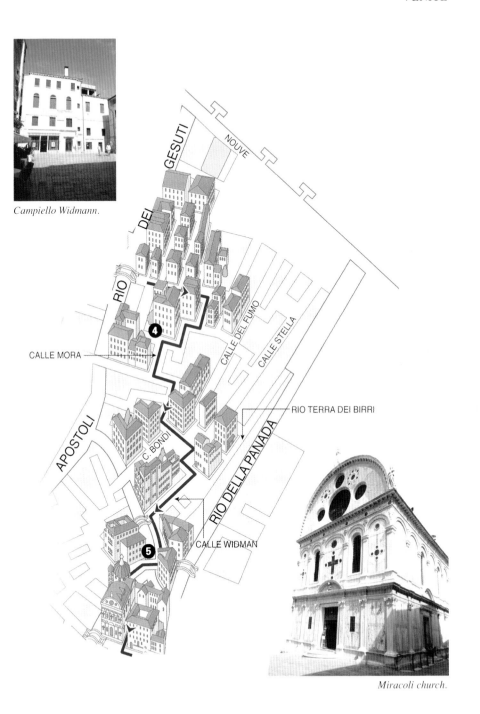

Campiello Widmann.

GESUTI

NOUVE

DEI

RIO

CALLE DEL FUMO

CALLE STELLA

❹

CALLE MORA

APOSTOLI

RIO TERRA DEI BIRRI

C. BONDI

RIO DELLA PANADA

CALLE WIDMAN

❺

Miracoli church.

*Palazzo
Van Axel.*

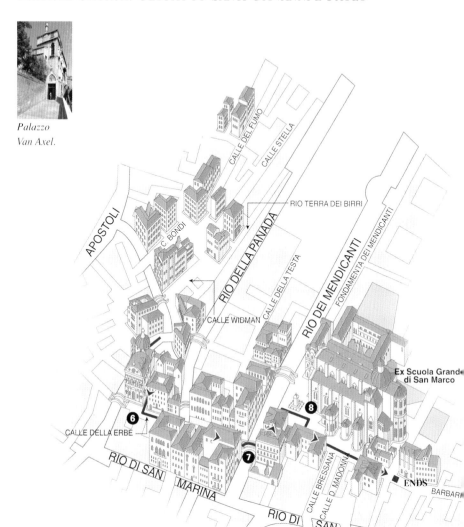

Calle Castelli.

6 From the church, take **Calle Castelli**, turning right on to **Fondamenta Van Axel** (turning left would take you to the *palazzo* of the same name). Though used as a national pavilion during the Venice Biennale and for occasional events, unfortunately this beautifully preserved *palazzo* is not usually open to the public. Over **Ponte delle Erbe** and down **Calle delle Erbe** you witness an unusual sight: the boundary of two Venetian districts. On one side of **Ponte Rosso** a sign says that Cannaregio ends here and on the other is a notice stating that you have reached the end of Castello.

Church of Santi Giovanni e Paolo.

Rio dei Mendicanti and the Scuola Grande .

7 From Ponte Rosso, turn left into **Campo Santi Giovanni e Paolo**, where two amazing sights stand side by side.The first is the **Scuola Grande di San Marco**, sometime confraternity and now the entrance to the Ospedale Civile (Venice General Hospital). Built by Pietro Lombardo and Giovanni Buora, it was completed by Mauro Codussi in 1495. The *scuola* was recently restored by Save Venice. It is possible to visit the library in the hospital and marvel at its 16thC carved ceiling; you may also want to visit the hospital chapel, containing a Tintoretto and a Veronese.

The second sight is the gargantuan **Santi Giovanni e Paolo**. The church was founded by the Domenican order in the 13th century, though the current building was not finished until nearly 200 years later. Its vast interior is a single spatial unit, made possible by the intricate cross-vaulting and tie beams. Many doges are buried here and, like the Frari, it contains chapels and monuments to Venetian patrician families. There is a profusion of great art, with works by Lorenzo Lotto, Cima da Conegliano and a polyptych by Giovanni Bellini in its original frame. The Lombardo family features once again, with a monument to Pietro Mocenigo.

Ospedaletto in Barbaria de le Tole.

8 In the *campo* opposite the church is **Rosa Salva**, serving delicious pastries and coffees beside the equestrian monument to Bartolomeo Colleoni, a 15thC *condottiere*. It is the work of Florentine sculptor Andrea Verrocchio. From the square, go down **Barbaria de le Tole** until you reach the **Ospedaletto**. Originally built as a hospice for the elderly and to house orphan girls, Santa Maria dei Derelitti, to give it its proper title, is still an old people's home. The façade is by Longhena and the interior includes works by Tiepolo. To reach the Ospedale *vaporetto* stop you can either continue down this street, turning left into **Calle delle Moschette**, or return to the *campo* and walk down the decidedly more picturesque **Fondamenta dei Mendicanti**.

Marco Polo Heartland: Rialto to San Zaccaria

► STARTS

Campo San Bartolomeo.
Nearest *vaporetto* stop:
Rialto.

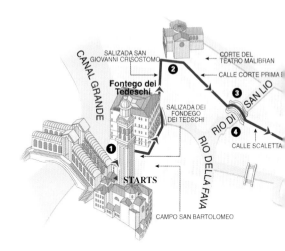

This is one of the guide's liveliest routes. Starting at the foot of the Rialto Bridge, you have to brave the hordes to reach some hidden treasures; then you are thrown back again into the seething crowds. But it's worth your while. The first port of call is Venice's main post office, which – like the city's general hospital – is no ordinary public building, but something of a spectacle. From there you make your way to the Teatro Malibran. Just around the corner is a *corte* that was home to Marco Polo, one of Venice's most illustrious sons.

Next you walk through an especially serene square before arriving at Campo Santa Maria Formosa, which is rarely quiet, and for good reason. It boasts dazzling *palazzi*, a delightful church, a museum celebrating both the city's past and contemporary art's present, and many a bustling bar and market stall. The last stretch of the route leads to the church of San Zaccaria, whose façade is a work of art, but whose Bellini painting inside is the true climax of this walk.

Campo Santi Filipo e Giacomo.

Ponte Marco Polo.

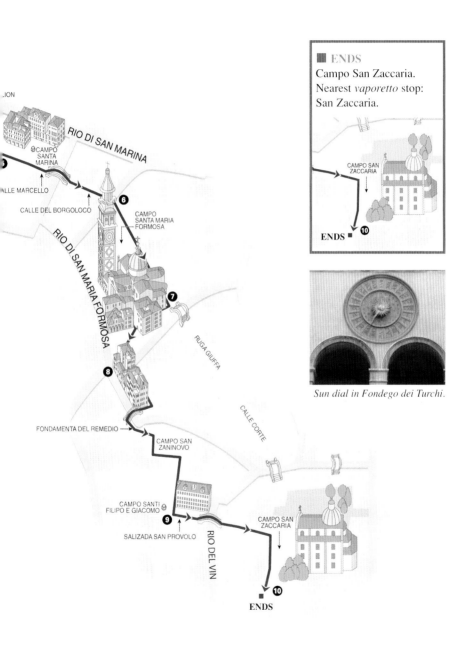

■ ENDS
Campo San Zaccaria.
Nearest *vaporetto* stop:
San Zaccaria.

CAMPO SAN
ZACCARIA

ENDS ■ ❿

Sun dial in Fondego dei Turchi.

RIO DI SAN MARINA

CAMPO
SANTA
MARINA

ALLE MARCELLO

CALLE DEL BORGOLOCO

❻

CAMPO
SANTA MARIA
FORMOSA

RIO DI SAN MARIA FORMOSA

❼

RUGA GIUFFA

❽

CALLE CORTE

FONDAMENTA DEL REMEDIO

CAMPO SAN
ZANINOVO

CAMPO SANTI
FILIPO E GIACOMO

❾

SALIZADA SAN PROVOLO

RIO DEL VIN

CAMPO SAN
ZACCARIA

❿

ENDS

95

❶ Starting with the **Rialto Bridge** behind you, and the shops of **Campo San Bartolomeo** ahead, take the first left into **Ramo del Fondego dei Turchi**. This short street has a well-stocked wine shop, **Mille Vini**, and a friendly bar serving some of the best sandwiches in the neighbourhood (**Osteria all'Alba**, closed Tue am; Sun pm). Directly ahead is the side entrance to the main post office. The

Rialto Bridge.

Fontego dei Tedeschi was leased to the German community as their trading centre and residential base in the 13th century. Titian and Giorgione frescoed the present 16thC building, though sadly their works can no longer be viewed here. Leaving the post office from the main entrance takes you into **Salizada dei Fondego dei Tedeschi**, with the lively nightspot **Bacaro Jazz** serving cocktails into the small hours. Crossing **Ponte de l'Olio** leads directly to Venice's only department store, **Coin**. Carry on down **Salizada San Giovanni Crisostomo** until you reach the eponymous church designed by Codussi and dedicated to the Archbishop of Constantinople. Works by Giovanni Bellini, Sebastiano del Piombo and Tullio Lombardo grace its three altars.

❷ Follow the church around into **Calle Corte Prima del Milion** and you will notice **Libreria Marco Polo**, which offers an ingenious multilingual book exchange service. Take the street to the right of the bookstore and enter **Corte del Teatro Malibran**. The **Teatro Malibran** was built in 1678 on the site of Marco Polo's family home. Of the many theatres in Venice, the Malibran was the first to open its doors to ticket-toting patrons, rather than maintain the strictly patricians-only policy of its competitors. Originally named after the nearby church, in 1835 the Teatro San Giovanni Crisostomo changed its name to honour Maria Garcia Malibran, the Spanish soprano who died tragically young in a riding accident in Manchester. More recently, the Malibran acted as the city's main theatre during La Fenice's laborious reconstruction.

Detail of carved archway.

3 Towards the back of the theatre is an archway intricately sculpted with various animals and animal heads leading into **Corte Secondo del Milion**. The well head in the centre of the square appears in Visconti's *Death in Venice*, with a weeping Dirk Bogarde falling to pieces on it. The courtyard's name derives from Marco Polo's account of his travels with his father and uncle to the Far East, *Il Milione*. Legend has it that the three shabbily dressed men returned home after 24 years away, their shoddy garb concealing precious gems and coins. The now-wealthy Marco Polo could only think in millions and that's how the *corte* got its new name. Leaving the square under the **Sotoportego del Milion** you enter **Fondamenta del Teatro** and here you can see a plaque on the Malibran façade commemorating this most adventurous of Venetians.

Corte Secondo del Milion.

Plaque on theatre honouring Marco Polo.

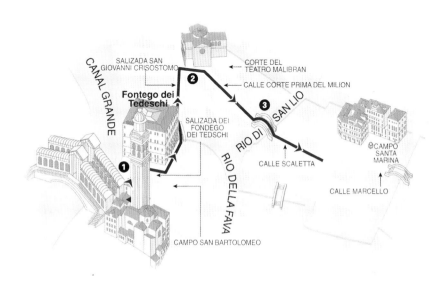

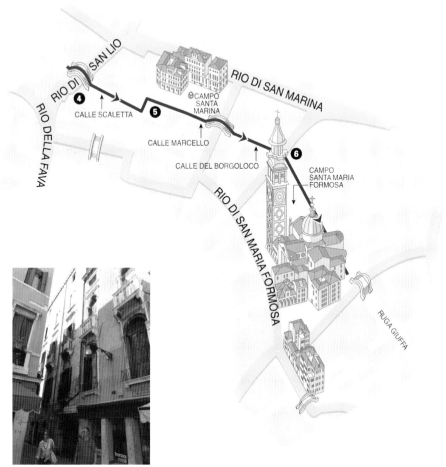

Campo Santa Marina.

❹ Ponte Marco Polo runs into **Calle Scaletta**, with the classy **Gabbiani** glass shop (closed Sun) overlooking the canal and street. At the end of the *calle*, turn left then right into the peaceful **Campo Santa Marina**. There are two excellent reasons for dawdling in this square, both of them culinary: the first is **Osteria di Santa Marina** (closed Sun, Mon lunch), serving creative fish dishes in a pristine and pretty setting; the second is **Pasticceria Didovich** (closed Sun), which offers sugary temptations such as individual lemon meringue pies. There's outdoor seating at both. Amazingly, for a city with such a profusion of churches, this square has none.

Campo Santa Marina.

Palace on Calle Borgoloco.

❺ Now you follow a mercifully straight line down **Calle Marcello**, also known as **Calle Pindemonte**, and over the bridge. Both names refer to the eminent owners of the palace situated at no. 6108 with a wonderful monumental façade attributed to Longhena. The Marcello family boasted a Doge (1473-74), and the Pindemonte clan could claim a noble lineage dating back to 1409. Continuing down **Calle del Borgoloco** (loosely meaning 'board and lodging', and allegedly so-called after the various hostelries once in the area), cross the bridge into **Ramo Borgoloco**.

Slot for offering money to the Blessed Virgin of the Birth.

❻ Before you is the capacious **Campo Santa Maria Formosa** (literally 'Curvaceous Saint Mary Square'). This bustling *campo* has exits leading to all parts of the city and is full of people traversing its vast expanse. It has a church designed by Codussi, which contains the celebrated painting of *St Barbara*, patron saint of soldiers, by the prolific Venetian artist Palma il Vecchio. Check out the hideous features of the face on the base of the *campanile*. Also in the *campo* are prestigious palaces formerly owned by some of Venice's most powerful patrician families, including the imposing **Palazzo Malipiero** (no. 5246), the top floor of which is now occupied by Warwick University, and the intricate Veneto-Byzantine **Palazzo Vitturi** (no. 6125). At the north end of the *campo* is **Zanzibar**, a fun little bar-kiosk popular with students, possibly due to its night-owl opening hours.

Church on Campo Santa Maria Formosa.

7 At the southern end, next to Palazzo Malipiero, is **Palazzo Querini Stampalia**. This historic family residence, along with its impressive art collection, was bequeathed to the city by Giovanni Querini in the 1800s with the condition that it be turned into a foundation and the library be opened 'for the convenience of scholars'. Thanks to Querini, students from around the world can be found beavering away at their books and laptops in the first-floor library. The museum contains period paintings and furniture, giving visitors an idea of patrician life in the 18th century. There is also a fine example of modern architecture by Venetian Carlo Scarpa, who created the Japanese-inspired garden and ground floor. Contemporary art exhibitions are held here, including the prestigious *Furla for Art* show.

Campo Santa Maria Formosa.

Southern end of Campo Santa Maria Formosa.

8 Leaving Palazzo Querini Stampalia, take the wide bridge to the right of the palace. **Ponte Pasqualigo e Avogardo** descends on to the camera-friendly **Fondamenta del Remedio**, with a cluster of private bridges and pretty palaces adorned with colourful geraniums. Walking under **Sotoportego de la Stua**, you reach **Campo San Zaninovo** (S. Giovanni in Oleo), with its modest bare-brick façade. The first church was built under the auspices of the powerful Trevisan family in the 10th century, though the present church dates back to the 1400s.

Fondamenta del Remedio.

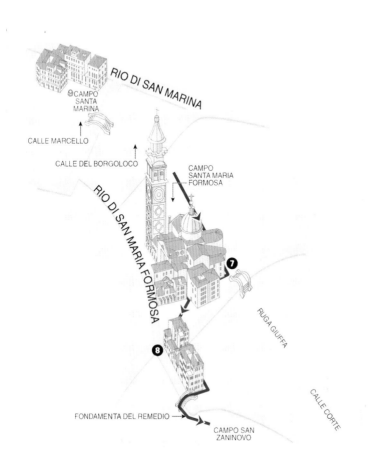

RIO DI SAN MARINA

CAMPO SANTA MARINA

CALLE MARCELLO

CALLE DEL BORGOLOCO

RIO DI SAN MARIA FORMOSA

CAMPO SANTA MARIA FORMOSA

❼

RUGA GIUFFA

❽

CALLE CORTE

FONDAMENTA DEL REMEDIO

CAMPO SAN ZANINOVO

Fondamenta del Remedio.

Church of San Zaninovo.

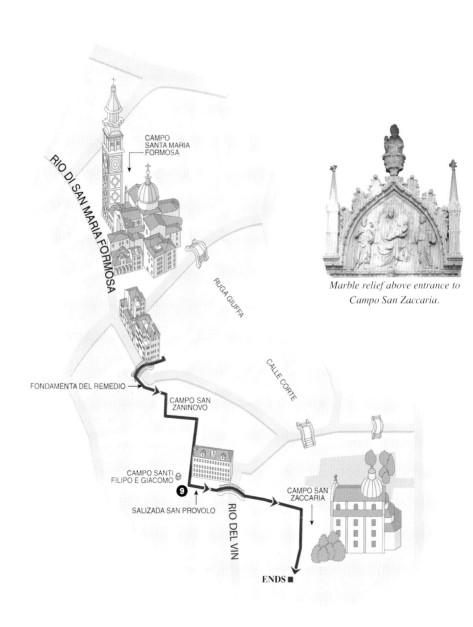

CAMPO SANTA MARIA FORMOSA

RIO DI SAN MARIA FORMOSA

RUGA GIUFFA

Marble relief above entrance to Campo San Zaccaria.

CALLE CORTE

FONDAMENTA DEL REMEDIO

CAMPO SAN ZANINOVO

CAMPO SANTI FILIPO E GIACOMO

9

SALIZADA SAN PROVOLO

RIO DEL VIN

CAMPO SAN ZACCARIA

ENDS ■

Street vendors in Campo Santi Filipi e Giacomo.

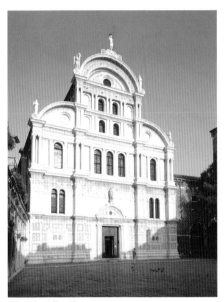

Church of San Zaccaria.

9 Following the church round, you find yourself just a hop, skip and a jump away from St Mark's Square in **Campo Santi Filipo e Giacomo**. This lively tourist spot is brimming with hotels and restaurants, not all of them good. An exception is **Aciugheta**, providing excellent pizzas and reasonably priced pasta in a buzzing atmosphere. The adjacent **Ridotto** (closed Wed, Thur lunch), under the same ownership, offers exclusivity and tranquillity along with its exemplary menu. Turning left from the *campo*, head down **Salizada San Provolo**, over the bridge and straight on, ducking under the magnificent marble portal leading into **Campo San Zaccaria**. As you enter, to your left note the marble edict against blasphemy, and the rowdy ball games often in progress here. Ahead of you is the **Church of San Zaccaria**, one of the most magnificent in the city. The body of St Zacharias, John the Baptist's father, was brought to Venice in the 9th century and lies under the second altar to the right. It was also the final resting place of a multitude of doges, as well as

containing a 10thC crypt. Remnants of a Romanesque mosaic floor are also testimony to the church's early foundation. The current building was built between the mid-1400s and the beginning of the following century; Mauro Codussi added a final flourish – the upper section of the façade. Among all the glut of ducal remains and holy artefacts is one outstanding work of art: Giovanni Bellini's sublime *Madonna and Child with Four Saints*. The adjoining convent once housed girls from the noblest houses in Venice and earned a reputation as a fashionable salon, rather than an austere religious academy. It was the abbess of the convent who first presented the Doge with his ducal cap, a tradition that was upheld for centuries. From this truly superlative church and square, you head south under **Sotoportego San Zaccaria,** where local folklore has it that conspirators killed Doge Pietro Tradonico in 836, until you reach the *vaporetto* stops.

Campo San Zaccaria.

Central San Marco: Sant'Angelo to San Samuele

Starting and ending on the Grand Canal, this walk penetrates the heart of the San Marco district, taking in half-forgotten churches, a defunct cinema and a phoenix rising from the flames. You will climb a spiral staircase tucked behind a curiously modern-looking square, and admire a private home-cum-museum. All things theatrical abound in this area, from the Museo Fortuny and La Fenice to the street names along the way. There are plenty of shopping opportunities and refreshingly little tourist tat. As you would expect from the Upper East Side (or Knightsbridge) of Venice, taste prevails, with antiques, fine paintings and lavish fabrics waiting to be bought by those with plenty of cash. Travellers with more modest means can view great art free in the awesome Chiesa di Santo Stefano, or, for a small fee, at François Pinault's Palazzo Grassi, where the walk ends.

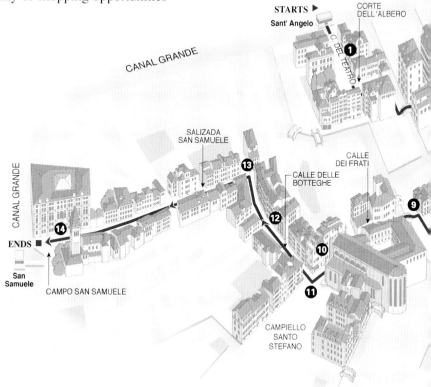

104

Gothic windows at Campo Manin.

Spiral staircase at Palazzo Contarini del Bovolo.

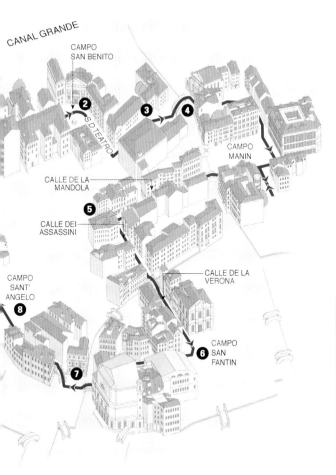

▶ **STARTS**
Sant'Angelo.
Nearest vaporetto
stop: Sant'Angelo.

■ **ENDS**
San Samuele.
Nearest vaporetto
stop: San Samuele.

1 The **Sant'Angelo** *vaporetto* stop is at **Campiello del Teatro**, so-called because of the theatre built here in 1676. Operas were mainly performed here until 1748, when the neighbouring Teatro di San Samuele burnt down, after which it was also used for plays. The *campiello* leads into **Corte dell'Albero**. Heading left out of the *corte* and then turning right, you

Fondamenta dell'Albero.

arrive on **Fondamenta dell'Albero**. Cross the bridge and go straight on down **Ramo Michiel** into **Calle Pesaro**, before crossing another bridge and reaching the end of the *calle*.

2 The small church in **Campo San Beneto** (St Benedict) was originally erected in 1005, though work on the present building began in 1619. In 1540, the original *campanile* toppled, destroying a quarter of the church under its rubble. The *campo* houses **Palazzo Pesaro**, now the **Museo Fortuny**. Once owned by the mighty Pesaro family, Mariano Fortuny bought the 15thC palace at the turn of the 20th century. Fortuny is famous for his sumptuous silks and other fabrics, but he was also a prolific set designer, photographer and costumier. The museum displays Fortuny dresses, textiles, paintings and photography. Temporary exhibitions are organized in this magical setting.

Leaving the *campo*, turn right into **Salizada del Teatro** and left into **Calle Sant'Andrea**, taking time to check out the pretty marble sculpture of the eponymous saint on the wall at no. 3981 in **Corte Sant'Andrea**. Continue down **Calle de le Muneghe** and under **Sotoportego de le Muneghe**. *Muneghe* is Venetian dialect for 'monks', and street names throughout the city remind one of its many convents and monasteries.

3 From here you reach the former **Teatro San Benedetto**, the principal theatre in Venice until it burned down in 1774. A spectacular ball was held at the theatre in 1780 to honour the visiting Russian princes, with a staging of *A Thousand and One Nights*. After its umpteenth revamp, the theatre was renamed the Rossini, in honour of the composer. Later, the theatre became Cinema Rossini, but it is now a desolate shell: the doors finally closed in 2003.

Campiello del Teatro.

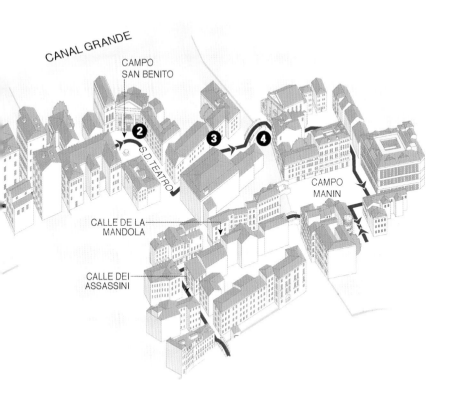

CANAL GRANDE

CAMPO SAN BENITO

S.D TEATRO

CALLE DE LA MANDOLA

CALLE DEI ASSASSINI

CAMPO MANIN

4 On the other side of **Ponte del Teatro** is the **Church of San Luca**. Beside the church, to the right, **Ramo a fianco la Chiesa** takes you into a *campiello*. Note the intriguing doorway at no. 4038 with a 13thC terracotta triangular pediment and coat of arms. Veering right, go down **Ramo de la Salizada** into **Campo Manin**, where a 1960s piece of architecture will surprise you. In the centre of the *campo* is a statue commemorating Daniele Manin, instigator of the 1848 uprising against the Austrians. Manin's gaze is fixed on his old home, on which a plaque is

Statue of Daniele Manin.

dedicated to him. Cross the square and head down **Calle de la Vida Bovolo** to **Corte Contarini**. Here you find the 15thC **Palazzo Contarini del Bovolo**: *bovolo* comes from Venetian for snail shell and refers to the building's stupendous external spiral stairway. The garden also boasts four Byzantine well heads. Return to Campo Manin and take the left-hand bridge, **Ponte de la Cortesia**, into the busy **Calle de la Mandola**, full of quirky stores such as the wonderful wool shop **Lellabella**, and the optician **Ottica Carraro** (closed Sun).

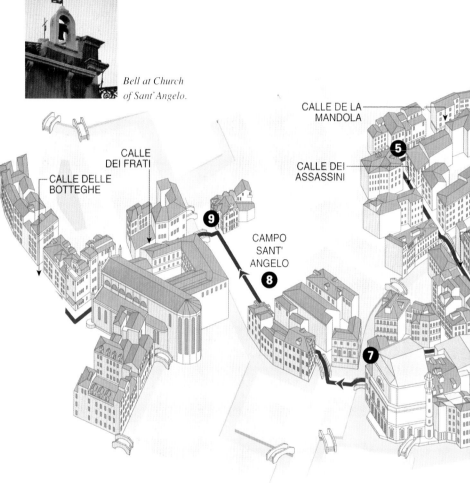

Bell at Church
of Sant'Angelo.

CALLE DE LA
MANDOLA

CALLE
DEI FRATI

CALLE DEI
ASSASSINI

CALLE DELLE
BOTTEGHE

CAMPO
SANT'
ANGELO

5 At the optician's, turn left into the sinisterly named **Calle dei Assassini**. Many stories circulate about how this street got its label. The main theory, not surprisingly, is that numerous murders were committed in the neighbourhood. Here you can find the postage-stamp store **Arte Casa** selling designer fabrics and household goods. Crossing **Rio Terà dei Assassini** you come upon the upmarket clothes store **Fabrizio Lenzi** (closed Sun). Continue down **Calle de la Verona**, over the bridge and past the **Venetia Studium** fabric and accessories showroom.

Campanile of
Santo Stefano.

Calle de la Verona.

Statues on top of Scuola di San Fantin.

6 Step out into **Campo San Fantin**. Its unassuming church houses a Renaissance apse by Jacopo Sansovino. Next to the church is the monumental **Scuola di San Fantin** and opposite is **Teatro La Fenice**, restored to its original splendour and reopened in 2004 after the devastating fire of 1996. This was not the first time the place had been in flames. In 1836, after an ominous performance of Rossini's *Cenerentola*, a fire devastated the theatre, leaving only the external walls and a pile of cinders. What you see now - guided tours are available - is a painstaking reconstruction of the ornate Baroque original: a monument not only to the past, but also to the craftsmanship of contemporary artisans. Facing the theatre, to your left, is pretty **Campiello San Gaetano**, with an external staircase.

CALLE DE LA VERONA

CAMPO
6 SAN
FANTIN

7 Walking down **Calle de la Fenice** to the right, turn left under **Sotoportego San Cristofero**. Cross the bridge on to a picturesque *fondamenta* and take the bridge to your right, **Ponte Storto**. From here, go down **Calle Caotorta**, named after one of Venice's original founding families.

Campo Sant'Angelo.

8 The street now opens on to **Campo Sant'Angelo**, with its startling view of the skewed *campanile* of adjacent Santo Stefano. Sant'Angelo is a pretty square, with a somewhat overrated but extremely popular eatery **Acqua Pazza** (closed Mon). Interesting *palazzi* include **Palazzo Duodo** at no. 3584, with its beautiful pointed-arch façade.

9 Here cross **Ponte dei Frati**, but not before popping into the tax office. This building (at no. 3538), situated on the bridge, has some stunning cloisters, having once been part of the Church of Santo Stefano, more of which below.

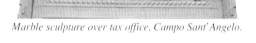

Marble sculpture over tax office, Campo Sant'Angelo.

10 Heading down **Calle dei Frati** from the bridge you reach the **Church of Santo Stefano**. Opposite the church is **Bar All'Angolo** (closed Sun), serving delicious sandwiches and snacks at fair prices. Discerning shoppers can drop into **Ebrú** for scarves and marbled, handcrafted paper. However, the church is why you are here and it is breathtaking. Similar in style and dimension to the Domenican Santi Giovanni e Paolo and the Franciscan Frari, the Church of Santo Stefano is Augustinian. Built in the 14th century, it has a wonderful marble portal, a ship's keel roof and a vast, gloomy interior. As well as two late Tintorettos, it contains a monument to the Venetian ambassador Giacomo Surian by Pietro Lombardo and sons.

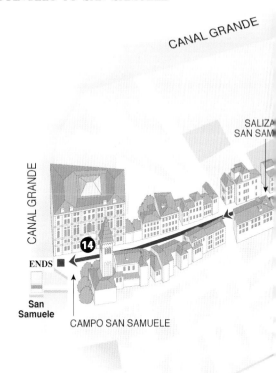

11 **Campo Santo Stefano** is a lively place, full of tourists at the outdoor tables and local kids racing around. It was even livelier in the past, with Venice's last bull fight held here in 1802. The deconsecrated **Church of San Vidal**, now a popular venue for concerts of Baroque music, is at the southern end of the *campo*, along with the monolithic **Palazzo**

Campo Santo Stefano.

Pisani, now home to Venice's prestigious conservatoire. In the middle of the square is a monument to Nicolò Tommaseo, a Dalmatian scholar who, like Daniele Manin, was an important figure in the uprising against the Austrians. Naughty Venetian schoolchildren refer to the statue as *Cagalibri* (Venetian dialect for 'book shitter'), for reasons that become obvious when looking at the back of it.

12 Leaving the *campo* at the northern end, head down the aptly named **Calle delle Botteghe** (Shop Street). Here you can find all manner of stores from the more prosaic baker's and hardware shops to antiquarians and luxury fabric boutiques. Of particular note are **Antiquus** (closed Sun), with a beautiful collection of old master paintings and jewellery, and **Gaggio** (closed Sat pm; Sun), whose silk velvets are legendary. Though fabrics are sold by the metre, you can also buy ready-made cushions, hats and jackets. Further down the street is the **Holly Snapp** art gallery (closed Sun) to the left and on the right is **Bacaretto** (closed Sun), open for excellent bar snacks and traditional Venetian food.

CALLE DEI FRATI

CALLE DELLE BOTTEGHE

CAMPIELLO SANTO STEFANO

Sculpture over entrance to the Church of Santo Stefano.

13 Turning left down **Salizada San Samuele** is the great interior design store **Guadagni** (closed Sun) with a range of exquisite fabrics. If you have the correct measurements, curtains and blinds can be made and sent to you. From here until you reach your goal, there are many galleries, with wood, glass and painting all well represented.

14 If you don't feel overdosed on art, you are now in for a treat. At the end of this long alleyway is **Campo San Samuele** and the mammoth 18thC **Palazzo Grassi**. Once owned by the beleaguered Fiat company, the palace was bought by François Pinault in 2005 and much of his private collection can be viewed here, including some Damian Hirst cows in formaldehyde and wicked works by Jeff Koons. Don't consider the walk over until you have taken a seat in the *campo* and enjoyed its entrancing view of the Grand Canal.

Palazzo Grassi.

Saints all the Way: San Giovanni in Bragora to San Francesco della Vigna

This is another lively route on which you will encounter tourists making their way to nearby St Mark's Square and the Bridge of Sighs. You'll wade through the hustle and bustle of street sellers flogging fake Fendi alongside *bona fide* vendors of kitsch souvenirs. If you are prepared to mingle with these crowds for part of the walk, you will be rewarded with some of the major attractions in Venice, as well as a handful of lesser-known delights. As the title suggests, this route leads you from one saint to another, commemorated in unspoilt *campi*, dozens of churches, an ex-monastery and a prestigious Venetian *scuola*. Though inevitably more crowded in parts because of its proximity to Piazza San Marco, this walk still explores a few peaceful paths. Highlights include the site of Vivaldi's baptism, the Greek Orthodox Church and a hidden *corte* believed to hold special powers, at least by local school kids. The route ends in the blissfully quiet and unworldly cloisters of celestial San Francesco della Vigna.

Façade of Scuola di S. Giorgio degli Schiavoni.

Cloister of S. Francesco della Vigna.

▶ STARTS
Riva degli Schiavoni.
Nearest *vaporetto* stop:
Arsenale or San
Zaccaria.

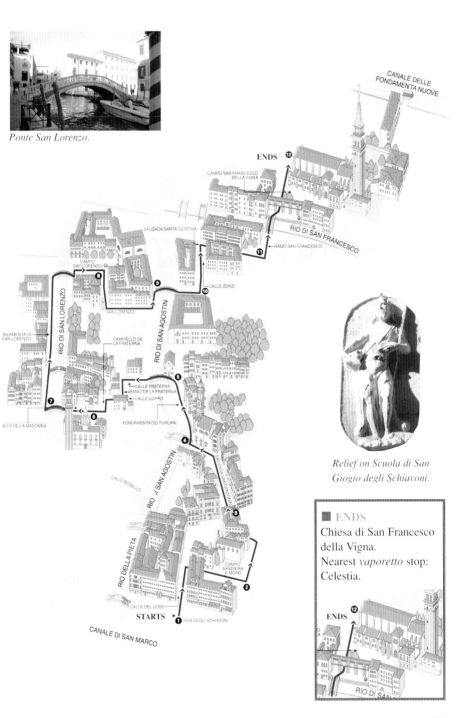

Ponte San Lorenzo.

CANALE DELLE FONDAMENTA NUOVE

ENDS **12**

CAMPO SAN FRANCESCO DELLA VIGNA

SALIZADA SANTA GIUSTINA

RIO DI SAN FRANCESCO

11 ← RAMO SAN FRANCESCO

CAMPO SAN LORENZO

8

9

CALLE ZORZI

10

SAN LORENZO

RIO DI SAN LORENZO

RIO DI SAN AGOSTIN

CAMPIELLO DE LA FRATERNA

FONDAMENTA DI SAN LORENZO

CALLE FRATERNA
RAMO DE LA FRATERNA
CALLE COPRO

5

7

6

ALLE DE LA MADONNA

FONDAMENTA DEI FURLANI

4

CALLE BOSELLO

RIO DI SAN AGOSTIN

SALIZADA SANT ANTONIN

3

CAMPO BANDIERA E MORO

2

RIO DELLA PIETA

CALLE DEL DOSE

STARTS ► **1** RIVA DEGLI SCHIAVONI

CANALE DI SAN MARCO

Relief on Scuola di San Giogio degli Schiavoni.

■ **ENDS**
Chiesa di San Francesco della Vigna.
Nearest *vaporetto* stop: Celestia.

ENDS **12**

RIO DI SAN

Saints all the Way: San Giovanni in Bragora to San Francesco della Vigna

❶ Starting on congested **Riva degli Schiavoni**, between San Zaccaria and Arsenale *vaporetto* stops is **Calle del Dose**. In the 16th century a pharmacy by the name of *Dose* plied concoctions at the corner of this street, and the name stuck.

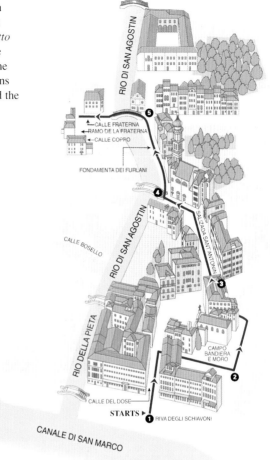

Calle del Dose.

Marble sculpture of St George and the Dragon in Campo Bandiera e Moro.

❷ The *calle* opens out on to **Campo Bandiera e Moro**, which houses the **Church of San Giovanni in Bragora**. Little is known about the origins of its name: *bragora* is believed by some to derive from the Venetian *bragola* (market square) and by others from the Greek *agorà*, meaning square. There are also doubts about the original church on this site. The first may have been built as early as the 8th century and was dedicated to John the Baptist, whose relics were stored here in the 9th century. The present Gothic structure dates from the 1400s. Treasures inside include *The Baptism of Christ* by Cima da Conegliano and a wonderful triptych by Bartolomeo Vivarini. Vivaldi, who was born in Campo Bandiera e Moro, was baptised here, as is shown by the official register on display.

3 Taking the right-hand exit out of the square past the imposing Gothic façade of **Palazzo Gritti** (no. 3608), turn left on to **Salizada Sant'Antonin**. On the left of this lively street is **Pasticceria Alla Bragora** (closed Mon), where you can raise your sugar level, and **Buena Onda** (closed Sat) where you can have a pick-me-up. In 1819, the **Church of Sant'Antonin**, whose foundation dates back to the 7th century, provided refuge for an elephant that had escaped from the zoo on Riva degli Schiavoni. Unfortunately, the story does not have a happy ending: the animal was shot by the local constabulary.

Marble sculpture on Church of Sant' Antonin.

4 Once past the church, veer right up **Fondamenta dei Furlani** to the **Scuola di San Giorgio degli Schiavoni**. The Schiavoni were the Slav population, their numbers growing exponentially so that at the end of the 1400s they were able to erect a *scuola* alongside the **Church of San Giovanni di Malta** (not open to the public). This building houses Carpaccio's stunning sequence of paintings depicting the lives of the Dalmatian saints Jerome, George and Tryphone, which he began in 1502. Make sure you visit the meeting room on the first floor.

Scuola di San Giorgio degli Schiavoni.

5 Leaving the *scuola*, cross **Ponte de la Commedia** (named after one of the neighbourhood theatres) and head straight into **Calle Fraterna**. The name comes from a religious establishment in the area that provided food and shelter for the homeless. Turn left into **Ramo de la Fraterna**, which leads into **Calle Coppo** and **Campiello de la Fraterna**. Just to the south of this tiny square, on the corner of **Calle Bosello**, is the famous **Trattoria Da Remigio** (closed Tue) serving classic Venetian fish dishes. Next door is **Osteria Oliva Nera**, boasting two restaurants, one specialising in fish (closed Wed), the other mainly meat (closed Thur). Continuing down Calle Bosello would lead you to the Pietà church, where Vivaldi once conducted. However, you should head west down **Calle de la Madonna**. On your right is the perfectly restored 14th century Gothic **Palazzo Zorzi-Liassidi**, now a luxury hotel. The Liassidi family, which owned the palace until the early 20th century, was from Cyprus, and the original owners, the Zorzi-Cornaro family, also had Cypriot links. One of their clan, Caterina Cornaro, became no less than Queen of Cyprus (1474-89) after marrying James the Bastard, the illegitimate son of John II of Cyprus.

Saints all the Way: San Giovanni in Bragora to San Francesco della Vigna

6 At the end of the *calle*, to the left, is the entrance to the **Museo dell'Istituto Ellenico** and the adjacent **Church of San Giorgio dei Greci**. After the Turks captured Constantinople in 1453, refugees flooded into Venice and this church and school of Hellenic studies has been part of the Venetian landscape since then. Treasures in the museum include a 14thC Byzantine cross.

7 From **Ponte dei Greci** turn right on to the pretty **Fondamenta di San Lorenzo**. At the foot of the bridge is **Bar Crazy**, where you can take a break, and just to your right is **Trattoria da Giorgio** where you can sit outside and enjoy the view of the church and its wonky *campanile*. At the end of this pleasant stretch is the police headquarters, or *Questura*. Towards the far end of the *fondamenta* is **Ponte di San Lorenzo**, leading into the eponymous square. Opposite is the immense brick façade of the church, and to your left is the Benedictine convent. The local patrician Partecipazio family paid for the church and a female family member, Romana, founded the nunnery. Now the church is closed and derelict and the Benedictine nuns are long gone. In their place are local residents of an old folks' home. And while the church steps were traditionally synonymous with charitable donations, at San Lorenzo beggars have been replaced by stray cats, their homes kindly provided by the City Council and their food doled out by local cat lovers.

Church of San Lorenzo.

8 To your right is **Calle San Lorenzo**: follow it around the flank of the church before being expelled on to the **Fondamenta di San Lorenzo** once more. Under the columns to the left is the entrance to the church hall, used as a community centre.

Calle San Lorenzo.

9 Crossing **Ponte de la Corte Nova** leads you into the strange little courtyard of the same name. Though seemingly unremarkable, this square is believed to hold miraculous powers. During the plague that ravaged the Venetian population in 1630 (and subsequently), the inhabitants of this courtyard were apparently immune. During the heavy Austrian bombardments during the First World War, again the *Corte* remained intact, with no fatalities, and it was believed that the Madonna was once more offering her protection. In the little *sotoportego* leading out of the courtyard is a shrine in her honour and above the archway is an explanation of the events. Another curiosity is the pink marble square set amongst the paving slabs. Pupils on their way to the nearby high school superstitiously believe that treading on this stone is a sure sign they will be hauled up in front of the class for cross-examination by the teacher.

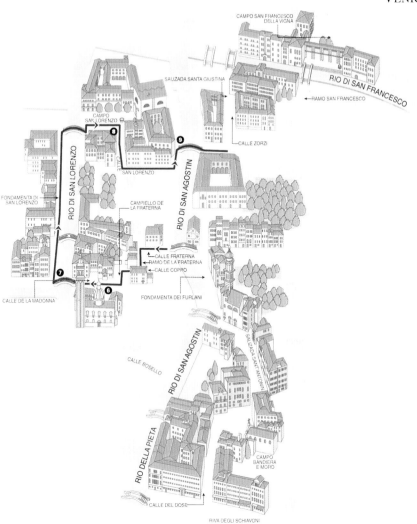

Shrine on Corte Nova.

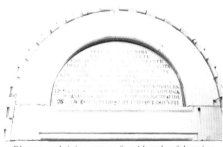

*Plaque explaining story of residents' safekeeping
thanks to the Blessed Virgin*

Saints all the Way: San Giovanni in Bragora to San Francesco della Vigna

Façade on Salizada Santa Giustina.

⓾ After ducking under the *sotoportego* – making sure you don't step on the inauspicious pink slab – head north up **Calle Zorzi**. At the top of the street on **Salizada Santa Giustina** is **Pizzeria 84** (open evenings only, closed Wed and Thur). Turning right finds you at no. 2926, **Palazzo Contarini**, its doorway topped with a 13thC marble arch and a 14thC relief bearing an angel and the family coat of arms. It is now divided into apartments, but if you are lucky (or polite and persistent with the residents), you may get to see the inner courtyard and its external staircase. On the corner of the street is a charming statue of the Virgin and Child on top of the wall, complete with a bronze umbrella to protect them from the elements.

⓫ Turning left at the statue into **Ramo San Francesco** and crossing the bridge finds you in **Campo San Francesco della Vigna**. Just a stone's throw away from the Arsenale, this northern square has maintained its local feel thanks to plenty of welfare housing and the nearby high school.

⓬ The few tourists that make it this far are here for the **Church of San Francesco della Vigna**. The name of this superlative church probably comes from the nearby vineyard (*vigna*) left to the friars in 1253. The church was designed by Sansovino and built in 1534. Andrea Palladio was responsible for the façade. The dark and sombre interior boasts some fine art. On the left of the chancel in the

Giustiniani Chapel are works by Pietro Lombardo and his school, while the fourth chapel to the right has a *Resurrection* by Paolo Veronese. To the left is a side door leading to the Cappella Santa (Holy Chapel), which contains a *Madonna and Saints* by Giovanni Bellini. But the best surprises are the two Renaissance cloisters secreted behind the church (there is a third, containing a vegetable garden, not open to the public). After your walk, often through busy streets, this peaceful place invites you to contemplate what you've seen.

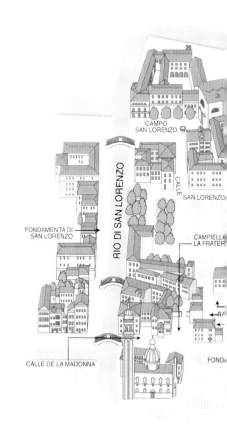

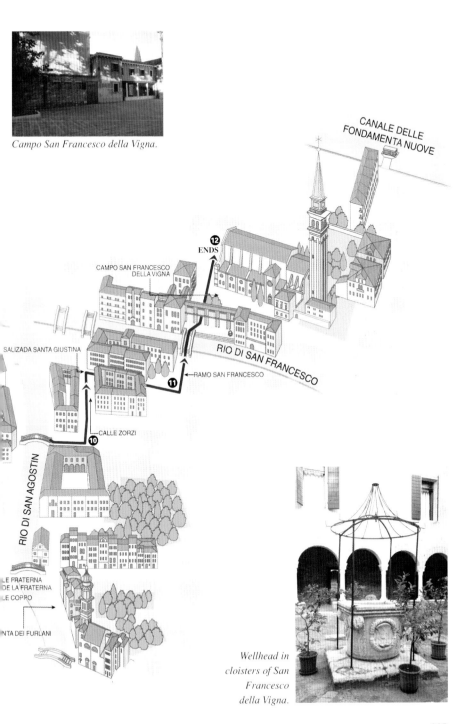

Campo San Francesco della Vigna.

CANALE DELLE FONDAMENTA NUOVE

12 ENDS

CAMPO SAN FRANCESCO DELLA VIGNA

SALIZADA SANTA GIUSTINA

RIO DI SAN FRANCESCO

RAMO SAN FRANCESCO

11

CALLE ZORZI

10

RIO DI SAN AGOSTIN

LE FRATERNA
DE LA FRATERNA
LE COPRO

NTA DEI FURLANI

Wellhead in cloisters of San Francesco della Vigna.

119

Green Venice: Giardini to San Pietro di Castello

This last walk in the guide begins in the calming surroundings of one of the city's few public green spaces: the Giardini Pubblici (Public Gardens). Not only is this part of town full of trees (the adjacent district of Sant'Elena provides another leafy haven), it is also one of the few

Giardini Pubblici.

'authentic' Venetian neighbourhoods in the city. Much of Venice has been gentrified, the locals ousted to make room for outsiders, but the parts of Castello visited on this route remain essentially Venetian. It may, in common with similar neighbourhoods, lack sophistication, but it still contains wonderful architecture, quiet canal banks, many shrines (not to mention photo opportunities), and more than a few great places to eat, drink and party. The walk winds up at San Pietro di Castello, home to the original Venice Cathedral and neighbouring Bishop's Palace, situated at a solitary tip of this island city.

Fondamenta Riello.

► STARTS
Giardini Pubblici.
Nearest *vaporetto* stop:
Giardini.

■ ENDS
Campo San Pietro di Castello.
Nearest *vaporetto* stop:
San Pietro.

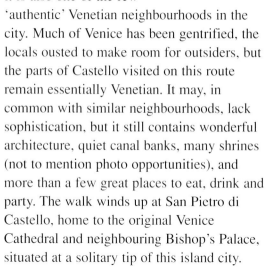

Giardini Pubblici.

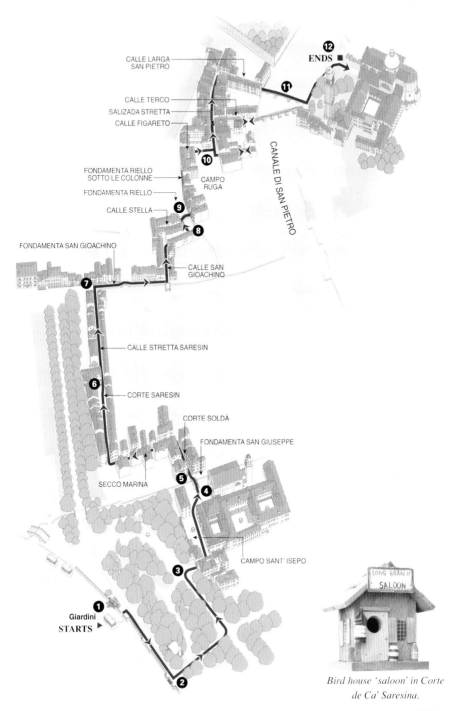

CALLE LARGA
SAN PIETRO

CALLE TERCO

SALIZADA STRETTA

CALLE FIGARETO

FONDAMENTA RIELLO
SOTTO LE COLONNE

FONDAMENTA RIELLO

CALLE STELLA

FONDAMENTA SAN GIOACHINO

CALLE SAN
GIOACHINO

CAMPO
RUGA

CANALE DI SAN PIETRO

ENDS

CALLE STRETTA SARESIN

CORTE SARESIN

CORTE SOLDÀ

FONDAMENTA SAN GIUSEPPE

SECCO MARINA

CAMPO SANT' ISEPO

Giardini
STARTS

*Bird house 'saloon' in Corte
de Ca' Saresina.*

Green Venice: Giardini to San Pietro di Castello

❶ Arriving at the **Giardini** *vaporetto* stop on **Riva dei Partigiani**, one of the first things you see – at least when the tide is low – is the bronze monument to the women partisans who died in the Second World War. Bordering the waterfront are the leafy **Giardini Pubblici**, site of the Venice Biennale, the huge international art exhibition held every two years from June to October. Inside the vast gardens, behind the public park to the right, national pavilions host works by their chosen artist. Recent representatives for the U.K. include Chris Ofili, Gary Hume and Tracy Emin. In intervening years is the Architecture Biennale – for more information see www.labiennale.org. The wisteria-clad **In Paradiso** (closed Mon) dishes up snacks and art in these lush surroundings.

Female Partisan statue at Giardini.

❷ With the playground to your right, enter the park and notice the statue of Conte Francesco Querini, replete with marble Siberian huskies and sledge. In 1899, along with ten other Italian explorers and a Norwegian crew, Querini set sail for the North Pole from Oslo on the *Stella Polare*, a converted whaler. Three teams left the base, each heading for the Pole, but Querini's team didn't make it to their destination and were never seen again, perishing in the harsh, icy wilderness.

Statue of Francesco Querini in Giardini.

❸ Taking the archway out of the back of the park finds you in **Rio Terà Sant'Isepo**, with **Campo Sant'Isepo** (Venetian vernacular for Santo Giuseppe - Saint Joseph) immediately to the left. The church was built in 1512 and an Augustine convent erected alongside, with the nuns imported from Verona. Later it was handed over to the Salesian nuns, but their convent is now the Venier Nautical Institute. Unfortunately the church is rarely open to the public, but if you are lucky enough to get inside, make sure you view Vincenzo Scamozzi's monument to Doge Marino Grimani (1595-1605).

Campo Sant'Isepo.

❹ Crossing the bridge takes you on to **Fondamenta San Giuseppe**. To the right of the bridge on this picturesque waterside is **Hostaria da Franz**. The original Franz arrived in Venice during the Austrian occupation and set up a bar selling wine and snacks out of his girlfriend's family's rope shop. Now Da Franz has changed into a classy seafood restaurant, with spit and sawdust a thing of the past.

Church of Sant'Isepo.

5 From the bridge, head straight down **Corte Soldà**, turning left into **Secco Marina**. Towards the end of the street, turn right into **Corte Saresin**. At the end of this wide residential street is a shrine to the Blessed Virgin and Saint Francis containing plastic flowers, necklaces and rosaries offered by locals. There is also an old black and white photo showing local women at work in front of the shrine.

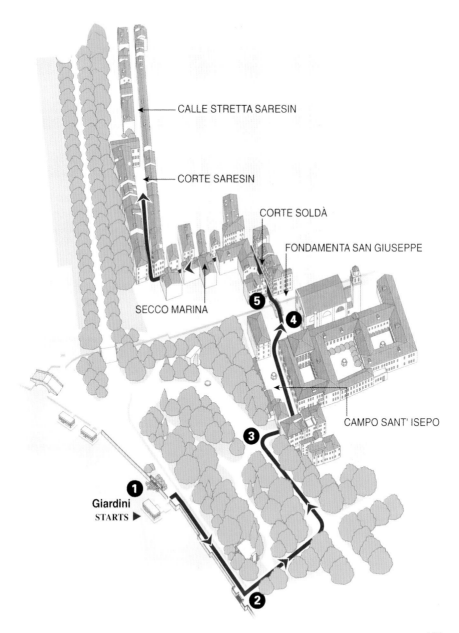

CALLE STRETTA SARESIN

CORTE SARESIN

CORTE SOLDÀ

FONDAMENTA SAN GIUSEPPE

SECCO MARINA

CAMPO SANT' ISEPO

Giardini
STARTS ▶

GREEN VENICE: GIARDINI TO SAN PIETRO DI CASTELLO

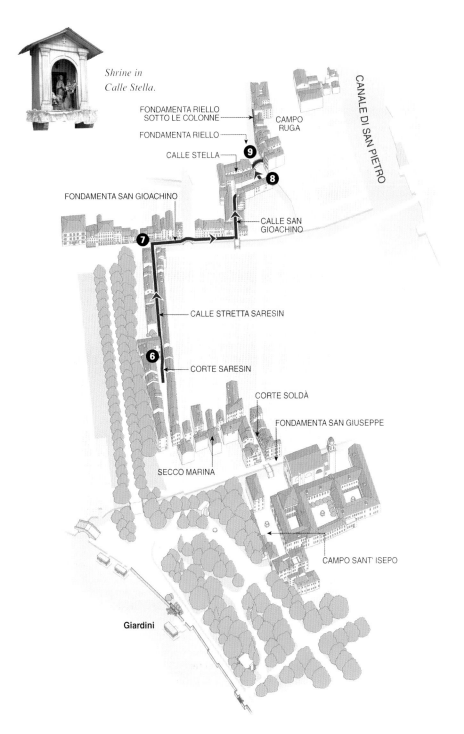

Shrine in Calle Stella.

FONDAMENTA RIELLO SOTTO LE COLONNE

CAMPO RUGA

FONDAMENTA RIELLO

CALLE STELLA

CANALE DI SAN PIETRO

FONDAMENTA SAN GIOACHINO

CALLE SAN GIOACHINO

CALLE STRETTA SARESIN

CORTE SARESIN

CORTE SOLDÀ

FONDAMENTA SAN GIUSEPPE

SECCO MARINA

CAMPO SANT' ISEPO

Giardini

Turbanned head doorknob in Calle Stretta de Ca' Saresina.

6 Heading past the shrine, through **Campiello Saresin** and **Calle Stretta Saresin**, checking out the fabulous turban-headed brass door handles on no. 1227, you reach bustling **Via Garibaldi**. Named after the great unifier of Italy, this wide thoroughfare is heaving with shops and market stalls, a sure sign that there is still a thriving local population. To your right is a floating fruit and vegetable shop. Opposite the barge is the friendly **Trattoria Alla Rampa** (closed Sun), serving *ombre* (small glasses of wine) and healthy portions of solid Venetian fare.

7 Swinging around the floating fruit takes you on to **Fondamenta San Gioachino**. From the bridge you have views of Rio San Daniele and the impressive Arsenale walls, which you will come across again later. On the *fondamenta* are the **Chiesetta e Casa di Santa Maria Ausiliatrice**, the latter once an orphanage for workers' children and now a play centre and temporary home to the Lithuanian Pavilion during the Biennale. To visit its simple cloisters, turn left down **Calle San Gioachino** and then left at the sign of the **Ludoteca La Luna nel Pozzo**.

Fondamenta San Gioachino.

8 From here, continue down the *calle* until you step out on to **Fondamenta Riello**. On sunny days, this *fondamenta* is packed to the gunwales with washing spanning the canal. Before crossing the bridge, take a quick detour under **Sotoportego Stella** and down **Calle Stella**. At the end of the alleyway is a quaint little shrine, and tucked away to its right is a private courtyard with a marble well head and marvellous Gothic windows incongruously situated on the ground floor.

Fondamenta Riello..

9 Retracing your steps back on to the *fondamenta*, cross **Ponte Riello**, turning left down the aptly named **Fondamenta Riello Sotto Le Colonne**. At the end of the columned canal bank is **Calle Figareto**. The name means 'little fig' and it is likely that fig trees were planted in the vicinity. The pretty *campiello* of the same name leads into **Campo Ruga**, an attractive square with park benches, for those in need of rest, and the welcoming **Trattoria Nuova Speranza** for sustenance. A concealed archway, **Sotoportego Zurlin**, leads into a Dickensian courtyard. However, after hunkering down in order to reach the *corte* and braving the gloom, the archway ahead offers a glimpse of your goal: the Canale di San Pietro and the island itself.

⑩ Retracing your steps once more, from the *sotoportego* turn right and head down **Salizada Stretta**. Should you fancy another detour, on the right **Calle Terco** leads into **Campiello Terco**, a delightful miniature square named after a wealthy Castello family. It offers wider views of the cathedral across the water. Towards the end of the street, turn right into **Calle Iarga San Pietro** to cross the wooden bridge over this vast expanse of water, taking time to admire the imposing Arsenale walls and turrets to the left.

Salizada Stretta.

Canale di San Pietro.

Anchors in the cloisters of San Pietro.

⑪ The island of **San Pietro di Castello** is thought to be one of the first inhabited islands of the lagoon, long before Venice came into being. Originally called *Olivolo*, possibly because of the bountiful olive groves there, it was later called *Castello* after a defensive castle was built there. Together with other islands, it formed the city of Venice and became its religious epicentre, with the Patriarch of Venice installed here from 1451. The shady *campo* has a few houses and at no. 69 there are some fragments of sculpture. The *campo* is also the venue for the *Festa di San Pietro*, which takes place at the end of June, and resembles a village fete-cum-barn-dance, with competitions, live music and traditional cooking.

⑫ The **Church of San Pietro** was once the cathedral of Venice and remained so until handing over the reins to the more ostentatious St Mark's in 1807. Codussi was responsible for designing the tilting stone *campanile* in 1482, and the church was built in 1557, following a design by wonder boy Palladio. Though somewhat forlorn inside, probably as a result of the two bombs it received during the Second World War, it holds a few gems, including *Saints John the*

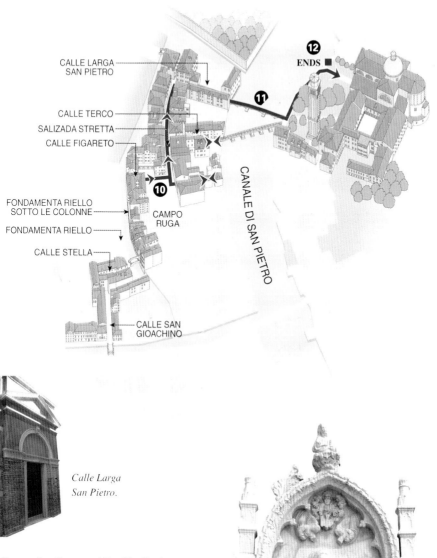

*Calle Larga
San Pietro.*

Evangelist, Peter and Paul by Paolo
Veronese. The main altar is by Salute
architect Longhena, but perhaps the most
unusual artefact is the Muslim funerary
stele from Antioch known as 'St Peter's
Throne'. After enjoying the peace of the
solitary **Campo San Pietro**, you reach the
vaporetto stop by following the path to the
left of the church.

Sculpture on Church of San Pietro.

Jo-Ann Titmarsh is a journalist and travel writer who lives in Venice. She loves walking and thinks the best way to see Venice is on foot.